HOW TO

ASSESS
HIGHER-ORDER
THINKING
SKILLS

IN YOUR CLASSROOM

ASCD MEMBER BOOK

Many ASCD members received this book as a
member benefit upon its initial release.

Learn more at: **www.ascd.org/memberbooks**

HOW TO

ASSESS
HIGHER-ORDER
THINKING
SKILLS

IN YOUR CLASSROOM

Susan M. Brookhart

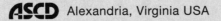 Alexandria, Virginia USA

1703 N. Beauregard St. • Alexandria, VA 22311-1714 USA
Phone: 800-933-2723 or 703-578-9600 • Fax: 703-575-5400
Web site: www.ascd.org • E-mail: member@ascd.org
Author guidelines: www.ascd.org/write

Gene R. Carter, *Executive Director;* Judy Zimny, *Chief Program Development Officer;* Nancy Modrak, *Publisher;* Scott Willis, *Director, Book Acquisitions & Development;* Genny Ostertag, *Acquisitions Editor;* Julie Houtz, *Director, Book Editing & Production;* Miriam Goldstein, *Editor;* Greer Wymond, *Senior Graphic Designer;* Mike Kalyan, *Production Manager;* Keith Demmons, *Typesetter;* Carmen Yuhas, *Production Specialist*

Printed in the United States of America. Cover art © 2010 by ASCD. ASCD publications present a variety of viewpoints. The views expressed or implied in this book should not be interpreted as official positions of the Association.

All Web links in this book are correct as of the publication date below but may have become inactive or otherwise modified since that time. If you notice a deactivated or changed link, please e-mail books@ascd.org with the words "Link Update" in the subject line. In your message, please specify the Web link, the book title, and the page number on which the link appears.

ASCD Member Book, No. FY11-1 (Sept., PSI+). ASCD Member Books mail to Premium (P), Select (S), and Institutional Plus (I+) members on this schedule: Jan., PSI+; Feb., P; Apr., PSI+; May, P; July, PSI+; Aug., P; Sept., PSI+; Nov., PSI+; Dec., P. Select membership was formerly known as Comprehensive membership.

PAPERBACK ISBN: 978-1-4166-1048-9   ASCD product #109111

Also available as an e-book (see Books in Print for the ISBNs).

Quantity discounts for the paperback edition only: 10–49 copies, 10%; 50+ copies, 15%; for 1,000 or more copies, call 800-933-2723, ext. 5634, or 703-575-5634. For desk copies: member@ascd.org.

Library of Congress Cataloging-in-Publication Data
Brookhart, Susan M.
  How to assess higher-order thinking skills in your classroom / Susan M. Brookhart.
     p. cm.
  Includes bibliographical references and index.
  ISBN 978-1-4166-1048-9 (pbk. : alk. paper) 1. Thought and thinking–Study and teaching (Secondary) 2. Critical thinking–Study and teaching (Secondary) 3. Cognition in children. I. Title.
  LB1590.3.B745 2010
    371.27'1–dc22
                                        2010018842

_____

20 19 18 17 16 15 14 13 12 11 10   1 2 3 4 5 6 7 8 9 10 11 12

HOW TO ASSESS
HIGHER-ORDER
THINKING SKILLS
IN YOUR CLASSROOM

Introduction 1

1. General Principles for Assessing Higher-Order Thinking 17

2. Assessing Analysis, Evaluation, and Creation 39

3. Assessing Logic and Reasoning 61

4. Assessing Judgment 84

5. Assessing Problem Solving 98

6. Assessing Creativity and Creative Thinking 124

Afterword 142

References 150

Index 153

About the Author 159

 Introduction

How many times in your adult life have you needed to recall a fact immediately? Sometimes it's handy to have facts at your fingertips. When I cook I often use the fact that three teaspoons equal one tablespoon. To understand the TV news, it is helpful to know some geographical facts, like the names and locations of various countries.

But think about it. You almost *never* need to know these facts for their own sake. My goal in cooking is having the dish I'm preparing turn out to be tasty. Math facts are useful when I'm working on my checkbook, a plan or budget, or a school report. Spelling facts are handy when I'm writing something. In life, almost everything we do requires *using* knowledge in some way, not just *knowing* it.

I believe that most teachers, in fact, do understand this reality. But we often don't carry it through into our assessment practices. Studies analyzing classroom tests, over many decades, have found that most teacher-made tests require only recall of information (Marso & Pigge, 1993). However, when teachers are surveyed about how often they *think* they assess application, reasoning, and higher-order thinking, both elementary (McMillan, Myron, & Workman, 2002) and secondary (McMillan, 2001) teachers claim they assess these cognitive levels quite a bit. Although some of this discrepancy may come from recent advances in classroom practices that emphasize higher-order thinking, it is also clear that many teachers believe they are assessing higher-order thinking when, in fact, they are not.

The reason that recall-level test questions are so prevalent is that they are the easiest kind to write. They are also the easiest kind of question to ask off the top of your head in class. Teachers who do not specifically plan classroom discussion questions ahead of time to tap particular higher-order thinking skills, but rather ask extemporaneous questions "on their feet," are likely to ask recall questions.

This situation is true for even the best teachers. After participating in professional development about questioning, one high school social studies teacher wrote the following:

> Upon reflection, it became obvious that many of the questions I have asked were at a lower-order thinking, or simply recall or factual response, level. [I am now . . .] more aware of the necessity for higher-order or open-ended questions in class. Many of the students also now understand the importance of the many different types of questions that can be asked.

The same thing happens on classroom tests. Teachers who put together tests quickly, or who use published tests without reviewing them to see what thinking skills are required, are likely to end up asking fewer higher-order-thinking questions than they intended. Contrary to some teachers' beliefs, the same thing also happens with performance assessments. Students can make posters or prepare presentation slides listing facts about elements, planets, or stars without using higher-order thinking, for example. Of course, what amount and what kind of higher-order thinking *should* be required on a classroom assessment depend on the particular learning goals to be assessed.

Most state standards and district curriculum documents list goals for learning that include both knowledge of facts and concepts and the ability to use them in thinking, reasoning, and problem solving. The purpose of this book is to clarify what is involved in several different aspects of higher-order thinking, and, for each, to show how to write good-quality, well-planned assessments.

What Is Knowledge?

The nature of human thought and reason is the subject of a field of philosophy called epistemology. Epistemologists still debate the definition of *knowledge*. A classic definition, based on ideas in Plato's dialogue *Theaetetus*, is that for something to count as knowledge it must be *justified*, *true*, and *believed*. Branches of philosophy have developed to describe what count as reasonable and plausible justifications, what counts as truth, and the nature of belief.

I use this tidbit about Plato to make what I consider an important point. Even seemingly simple knowledge rests on some historical higher-order thinking. Facts and concepts did not just fall out of the sky—or out of a textbook. They were discovered and debated until they came to be widely held as true, and widely believed. When we teach students to do higher-order thinking, we are not just teaching them some fancy skills useful for the flexibility and adaptability required for life in our 21st century "information age." We are teaching them to be human.

What Is Higher-Order Thinking?

If we agree to stay grounded in this important purpose, our definitions of higher-order thinking for the purposes of this book can be much more modest and practical. In this Introduction, we consider the kinds of higher-order thinking that are (or should be) stated or implied in state content standards and classroom learning objectives. Definitions that I find helpful fall into three categories: (1) those that define higher-order thinking in terms of *transfer*, (2) those that define it in terms of *critical thinking*, and (3) those that define it in terms of *problem solving*.

Here is a definition in the *transfer* category:

> Two of the most important educational goals are to promote retention and to promote transfer (which, when it occurs, indicates meaningful learning) . . . retention requires that students remember what they have learned, whereas transfer requires students not only to remember but also to make sense of and be able to use what they have learned. (Anderson & Krathwohl, 2001, p. 63)

The *critical thinking* category includes this definition:

> Critical thinking is reasonable, reflective thinking that is focused on deciding what to believe or do. (Norris & Ennis, 1989, p. 3)

Another example in this category comes from Barahal (2008), who defines *critical thinking* as "artful thinking" (p. 299), which includes reasoning, questioning and investigating, observing and describing, comparing and connecting, finding complexity, and exploring viewpoints.

In the *problem solving* category are these two definitions:

> A student incurs a problem when the student wants to reach a specific outcome or goal but does not automatically recognize the proper path or solution to use to reach it. The problem to solve is how to reach the desired goal. Because a student cannot automatically recognize the proper way to reach the desired goal, she must use one or more higher-order thinking processes. These thinking processes are called *problem solving*. (Nitko & Brookhart, 2007, p. 215)

> As you explore new domains you will need to remember information, learn with understanding, critically evaluate ideas, formulate creative alternatives, and communicate effectively. [A problem-solving] model can be applied to each of these problems . . . to help you to continue to learn on your own. (Bransford & Stein, 1984, p. 122)

Of course, the first thing that may strike you as you read these definitions is that there is a lot of overlap. In the discussion here, and in the chapters that follow, this overlap will be apparent as well. I discuss the definitions separately in the following sections and give practical advice for assessment of these different aspects of higher-order thinking in Chapters 2 through 6, for analytical reasons. As any taxonomy of higher-order thinking skills shows, pulling a concept apart and discussing its various aspects is one way of understanding it. Think of this book as an analysis of classroom assessment of higher-order thinking.

Higher-Order Thinking as Transfer

The most general of the approaches to higher-order thinking is the Anderson and Krathwohl (2001) division of learning into learning for *recall* and learning for *transfer*. Learning for recall certainly requires a type of thinking, but it is learning for transfer that Anderson, Krathwohl, and their colleagues consider "meaningful learning." This approach has informed their construction of the Cognitive dimension of the revised Bloom's taxonomy.

For many teachers, operating with their state standards and curriculum documents, higher-order thinking is approached as the "top end" of Bloom's (or any other) taxonomy: Analyze, Evaluate, and Create, or, in the older language, Analysis, Synthesis, and Evaluation (Anderson & Krathwohl, 2001). Chapter 2 discusses assessing higher-order thinking conceived of as the top end of a cognitive taxonomy.

The teaching goal behind any of the cognitive taxonomies is equipping students to be able to do transfer. "Being able to think" means students can apply the knowledge and skills they developed during their learning to new contexts. "New" here means applications that the student has not thought of before, not necessarily something universally new. Higher-order thinking is conceived as students being able to relate their learning to other elements beyond those they were taught to associate with it.

There is a sense in which teaching for transfer is a general goal of education. Many teachers use the phrase "What are you going to do when I'm not here?" Most of the time, this reflects teachers' appreciation of the fact that their job is to prepare students to go into the world ready to do their own thinking, in various contexts, without depending on the teacher to give them a task to do. Life outside of school is better characterized as a series of transfer opportunities than as a series of recall assignments to be done.

Higher-Order Thinking as Critical Thinking

Critical thinking, in the sense of reasonable, reflective thinking focused on deciding what to believe or do (Norris & Ennis, 1989) is another general ability that is sometimes described as the goal of teaching. In this case, "being able to think" means students can apply wise judgment or produce a reasoned critique. An educated citizen is someone who can be counted on to understand civic, personal, and professional issues and exercise wisdom in deciding what to do about them. As we all learned in American history class, Thomas Jefferson argued this point explicitly. He believed that education was necessary for freedom, that having a citizenry that could think and reason was necessary for a democratic government.

The goal of teaching here is seen as equipping students to be able to reason, reflect, and make sound decisions. Higher-order thinking means students can do this. One of the characteristics of "educated" people is that they reason, reflect, and make sound decisions on their own without prompting from teachers or assignments.

Wisdom and judgment are particularly important in higher-order thinking tasks like judging the credibility of a source, always an important skill but newly emphasized in the era of ever-expanding, electronically available information. Identifying assumptions, a classic skill, also is very relevant today. As school and society become increasingly diverse, it is less likely that everyone's assumptions will be similar. Identifying the assumptions behind points of view—what students might call "seeing where you're coming from"—is a true life skill.

Examples of the importance of critical judgment occur in all disciplines. Literary criticism involves both analyzing works of literature and evaluating to what degree the piece of writing succeeds in accomplishing the author's purpose. Advertisers estimate the effect of various advertising strategies on different audiences. Closer to home, students estimate the effects various arguments might have in persuading their parents of their point of view. All of these involve critical judgment about purposes and assumptions and about the relative effectiveness of various strategies used to meet these purposes.

To help students learn to think by looking at works of art, Project Zero at Harvard University developed the "Artful Thinking Palette" (Barahal, 2008). Six thinking dispositions are listed around the image of a paint palette: exploring viewpoints, reasoning, questioning and investigating, observing and describing, comparing and connecting, and finding complexity. Although these dispositions were developed in the context of learning from visual art, they are good ways to approach other critical-thinking tasks as well. For example, try thinking about how these six approaches apply in the study of literature, history, or science.

Higher-Order Thinking as Problem Solving

A problem is a goal that cannot be met with a memorized solution. The broad definition of *problem solving* as the nonautomatic strategizing required for reaching a goal (Nitko & Brookhart, 2007) can also be seen as a broad goal of education. Every academic discipline has problems. Some are closed problems, like a set of math problems designed to elicit repeated practice with a particular algorithm. But many problems are open-ended, could have many correct solutions or multiple paths to the same solution, or are genuine questions for which answers are not known. Economists, mathematicians, scientists, historians, engineers—all are looking for effective or efficient solutions to both practical and theoretical problems. Educators are, too. Teachers propose a solution strategy for a complex problem—how to effectively teach a particular learning target to particular students in a given amount of time and with the materials available—every time they write a lesson plan. Many life problems are open-ended. For example, planning for and living within a budget is an open-ended problem most households deal with. People solve problems in many different ways, depending on the values and assumptions they bring to the task.

Bransford and Stein (1984) noted that problem solving broadly conceived—in a model they call the IDEAL problem solver, which I'll describe in Chapter 5—is the mechanism behind learning for understanding. This is a similar position to Anderson and Krathwohl's (2001) discussion of "meaningful learning." Bransford and Stein also point out that problem solving is the general mechanism behind all thinking, even recall. This may seem ironic, but think of it this way. To recall something, students have to identify it as a problem ("I need to memorize the capitals of all 50 states. How can I do that?") and devise a solution that works for them.

In fact, Bransford and Stein say that in addition to driving both recall and learning, problem solving is necessary for critical thinking, creative thinking, and effective communication. The role of problem solving in critical thinking (for example, "How well did this movie director accomplish his purpose with this film?") and communication (for example, "How can I write this review so that readers will be interested in seeing the movie?") seems pretty obvious. But does problem solving have a role in creativity? Isn't creativity the free-spirit, whatever-you-want kind of thinking? Actually, no. Most human creations, both inventions of things and inventions of social customs, were conceived to solve some sort of problem. The proverbial invention of the wheel, for example, solves a problem that can be expressed as "How do I get this heavy stuff from here to there?"

If you think of higher-order thinking as problem solving, the goal of teaching is equipping students to be able to identify and solve problems in their academic work and in life. This includes solving problems that are set for them (the kind of problem solving we usually think of in school) and solving new problems that they define themselves, creating something new as the solution. In this case, "being able to think" means students can solve problems and work creatively.

What Is the Effect of Assessing Thinking Skills?

When you teach and assess higher-order thinking regularly, over time you should see benefits to your students. Your understanding of how your students are thinking and processing what they are learning should improve as you use assessments specifically designed to show students' thinking. Ultimately, their thinking skills should improve, and so should their overall performance. Students learn by constructing meaning, incorporating new content into their existing mental representations; therefore, improving thinking skills should actually improve content knowledge and understanding as well. How large can we expect this effect to be?

Higgins, Hall, Baumfield, and Moseley (2005) did a meta-analysis of studies of thinking-skills interventions on student cognition, achievement, and attitudes. A meta-analysis is a quantitative synthesis of studies that reports effect sizes, or amount of change in standard-deviation units. Standardizing the effects from different studies means researchers can average effect sizes across studies, which yields a more stable estimate of the size of an effect—in this case, the effect of thinking-skills interventions—than any one study alone could provide. For their review, Higgins and his colleagues defined thinking-skills interventions as "approaches or programmes which identify for learners translatable mental processes and/or which require learners to plan, describe, and evaluate their thinking and learning" (p. 7).

Higgins and his colleagues found 29 studies, from all over the world but mostly from the United States and the United Kingdom, that were published in English and that reported enough data to calculate effect sizes. Nine of the studies were conducted in primary schools and 20 in secondary schools; most were in the curriculum areas of literacy (7 studies), mathematics (9 studies), and science (9 studies). Their purpose in doing the meta-analysis was to estimate the size of effects of teaching and assessing thinking skills, and they found very strong effects. The average effect of thinking-skills instruction was as follows:

- 0.62 on cognitive outcomes (for example, verbal and nonverbal reasoning tests), over 29 studies.
- 0.62 on achievement of curricular outcomes (for example, reading, math, or science tests), over 19 studies.
- 1.44 on affective outcomes (attitudes and motivation), over 6 studies.

Because of the small number of effect sizes of motivational outcomes, the average effect size estimate of 1.44 may be less reliable than the other two effect sizes. But even 0.62 is a large effect for an educational intervention, equivalent to moving an "average" class of students from the 50th percentile to the 73rd percentile on a standardized measure.

Overall, then, Higgins and colleagues' meta-analysis supports the conclusion that thinking-skills interventions are effective in supporting student improvement in thinking, content area achievement, and motivation. In the next sections I describe some specific studies from the United States that support this conclusion. The studies described only scratch the surface of research in this area, and I encourage readers who are interested to look up additional works.

Assessing Higher-Order Thinking Increases Student Achievement

Using assignments and assessments that require intellectual work and critical thinking is associated with increased student achievement. These increases have been shown on a variety of achievement outcomes, including standardized test scores, classroom grades, and research instruments, as the studies described here illustrate. These increases have been demonstrated in reading, mathematics, science, and social studies. And they have been documented particularly for low-achieving students.

Evidence from NAEP and TIMSS. Wenglinsky (2004) reviewed studies of the relationships between student performance on large-scale measures and instruction emphasizing higher-order thinking, projects, and multiple-solution problems. He reported clear evidence from both the National Assessment of Educational Progress (NAEP) and the Trends in International Mathematics and Science Study (TIMSS) that, in mathematics and science, instruction emphasizing reasoning was associated with higher scores in all grade levels tested. In reading, teaching for meaning (including thinking about main ideas, author's purpose, and theme, and using real texts) was associated with higher NAEP performance as well, although Wenglinsky reminds his readers that NAEP testing begins in 4th grade, so it does not shed light on approaches to teaching beginning reading. In civics, 4th graders who studied basic information about how government works performed better on NAEP, but by 8th grade, students whose instruction also included active involvement and thinking did better.

Evidence from an urban district. Newmann, Bryk, and Nagaoka (2001) studied the mathematics and writing assignments of Chicago teachers in grades 3, 6, and 8. Students who received assignments requiring "authentic intellectual work" (p. 2) made greater-than-average gains in reading and mathematics on the Iowa Tests of Basic Skills (ITBS), and in reading, mathematics, and writing on the Illinois Goals Assessment Program (IGAP). As the name suggests, the ITBS is a basic skills test. The IGAP was the state test in place in Illinois at the time of the study.

To do their study, Newmann, Bryk, and Nagaoka had to define what they meant by "authentic intellectual work." They contrasted two kinds of instruction: didactic and interactive. By "didactic" instruction, they meant the kind of instruction in which students learn facts, algorithms, definitions, and such. In didactic instruction, students are tested with "right-answer," recall-level questions or with problems that require application or problem solving just like what was done in class.

However, in "interactive" instruction, "students are often asked to formulate problems, to organize their knowledge and experiences in new ways to solve them, to test their ideas with other students, and to express themselves using elaborated statements, both orally and in writing" (Newmann et al., 2001, pp. 10–11). Readers will hear in this definition the kind of higher-order thinking discussed in this book. In this kind of instruction, students are assessed with non-routine application of knowledge and skills. The researchers defined "authentic intellectual work" as requiring "construction of knowledge, through the use of disciplined inquiry, to produce discourse, products, or performances that have value beyond school" (p. 14). This kind of work was associated with one-year learning gains on the ITBS that were 20 percent greater than the national average. On the IGAP, students from classes that did this kind of work performed about half a standard deviation above students from classes whose work was very didactic. Students with both high and low prior achievement benefited.

Evidence for disadvantaged students. Pogrow (2005) designed the Higher Order Thinking Skills (HOTS) program specifically for educationally disadvantaged students, both Title I students and students with learning disabilities. The program specifically works on four kinds of thinking skills: (1) metacognition, or the ability to think about thinking; (2) making inferences; (3) transfer, or generalizing ideas across contexts; and (4) synthesizing information. In its 25-year history, the HOTS program has produced gains on nationally normed standardized tests, on state tests, on measures of metacognition, in writing, in problem solving, and in grade point average.

Two things make these results for the HOTS program particularly impressive. For one, in several of the evaluations, teaching thinking skills has been contrasted with enhanced content instruction. The thinking-skills instruction did a much better job of setting up the students to be flexible, allowing them to "understand understanding" (p. 70) and to handle all sorts of different content. For another, these results hold for about 80 percent of students who have been identified as Title I or learning disabled students, as long as they have a verbal IQ of 80 or above. It takes time, though. Pogrow (2005) reports that with these students, "It takes about four months before students will give a reason for a response without being asked, and it takes about six months before they will disconfirm a prior answer" (p. 71). But they do!

Assessing Higher-Order Thinking Increases Student Motivation

Studies have shown that holding students accountable for higher-order thinking by using assignments and assessments that require intellectual work and critical thinking increases student motivation as well as achievement. Students do not become engaged with their studies in the abstract, nor do they become motivated in the abstract. Rather, they become engaged in thinking *about* particular things and motivated to learn particular things. Higher-order thinking increases students' sense of control over ideas. Thinking is much more fun than memorizing.

A study of 3rd grade language arts. Meece and Miller (1999) studied elementary students' goal orientations (interest in mastery and interest in performing well), perceived competence, and strategy use in reading and writing. During the research project, some of the 3rd grade teachers expressed concern that their students showed mastery of skills and strategies on reading and writing tests but did not transfer those skills to actual reading and writing beyond the tests. Meece and Miller evaluated the 3rd grade assignments and found that most of them focused on individual skills, recall, and teacher control. Many assignments required one-word answers, for example. Meece and Miller helped teachers learn to devise assignments that required students to read extended material, write more than one paragraph, and collaborate with classmates. Students in classes where teachers gave these kinds of assignments regularly declined in their performance-goal orientation (meaning they were less inclined to want to do assignments for the sake of gaining the approval of others).

More interesting, work-avoidance scores of low-achieving students in these classes (from student questionnaires about schoolwork) decreased, whereas work-avoidance scores of low achievers in the regular classes stayed the same. This finding may seem like a conundrum. Arguably, work that required more reading and writing could have been more, not less, off-putting, especially to low achievers. But the opposite was the case. Low-achieving students were more motivated to do the thoughtful work than the one-word-answer drill work.

A study of 5th grade social studies. In a much smaller-scale study—but one very similar to something you could do in your own classroom—Carroll and Leander (2001) were concerned that their own 5th grade social studies students lacked interest in the topic and that many perceived it as difficult and not fun. Their master's thesis reported on a 14-week project to teach students learning strategies designed to improve higher-order thinking. They also instituted cooperative learning to allow students to think together.

Observations before the program suggested the average student was off-task during class about 20 percent of the time and inactive about 10 percent of the time. In a survey, less than half (47 percent) agreed that they were excited about learning, and less than half (47 percent) agreed that social studies assignments were easy. After a 14-week program that included teaching students questioning strategies, using graphic organizers, cooperative-learning research projects, and portfolio construction, the measures were repeated. This time, observations suggested the average student was off-task during class only about 10 percent of the time and inactive about 8 percent of the time. In the survey, 95 percent agreed that they were excited about learning, and 89 percent agreed that social studies assignments were easy. Students' grades on chapter-comprehension assignments improved as well.

A study of teacher and student perceptions of learner-centered practices. Meece (2003) reported on a study of 109 middle school teachers and 2,200 middle school students in urban, suburban, and rural communities. Both teachers and students completed surveys to assess the use of learner-centered teaching practices that stress higher-order thinking. For teachers, the only ratings correlated with student motivation and achievement were related to teachers' reported support for higher-order thinking. For students, ratings on all the learner-centered practice dimensions (including practices supporting higher-order thinking) were correlated with motivation and achievement. Higher-order thinking practices were the only practices found to be related to motivation from both teachers' and students' perspectives.

The Contents of This Book

This book is intended to help teachers assess the kind of complex thinking emphasized by current content standards in various disciplines. I first lay out principles for assessment in general and for assessment of higher-order thinking in particular (Chapter 1). Then I define and describe aspects of higher-order thinking emphasized in classroom learning and give examples of how to assess each aspect (Chapters 2 through 6).

The focus of the book is on *assessment* of higher-order thinking. I describe how to design assessments that require students to do higher-order thinking in an explicit enough form that the thinking becomes visible for appraisal, feedback, and discussion with the student. I describe both how to write and how to score questions and assessment tasks. The scoring is part of the assessment: if a question requires higher-order thinking but the scoring scheme only gives points for correct recall of facts, the assessment fails as a measure of higher-order thinking.

Of course, assessment of higher-order thinking assumes *teaching* of higher-order thinking. Although teaching these skills is not the subject of this book, it is worth noting that working through tasks like those in this book, with lots of feedback, could be part of such instruction. The ultimate goal is for students to learn to do more higher-order thinking, and do it better.

For ease of illustration, I use the following categories of higher-order thinking in the chapters illustrating ways to assess various aspects of such thinking:

- Analysis, evaluation, and creation (the "top end" of Bloom's taxonomy).
- Logical reasoning.
- Judgment and critical thinking.
- Problem solving.
- Creativity and creative thinking.

Chapters 2 through 6 describe in more detail the specific category, give guidelines for how to assess it, and provide some examples. These categories are consistent with the discussions of higher-order thinking as transfer, reasoned judgment, and problem solving. They also make a useful framework for talking about assessment (and instruction, too, for that matter), because slightly different strategies are used to assess each one. And as I have already said, there is overlap.

Throughout the book I have included many examples of assessments of higher-order thinking. The examples come from several sources. Some are particular examples that teachers have given me permission to share. Others are examples I have written myself that are based on many real examples but are not exact reproductions of any one of them. I have also used examples from NAEP because this is a good public source of well-written assessment items. The focus here is on individual items and tasks, not NAEP results or any of their uses in your state. This book is about classroom assessment of higher-order thinking.

Some readers may be surprised to see that some of the examples are multiple-choice test items. We often think of essays and performance assessments when we think of assessing higher-order thinking. But well-written multiple-choice items, especially those with introductory material, can also assess higher-order thinking. You wouldn't rely on multiple-choice items alone for such assessment, but it is important to be able to include on multiple-choice tests questions that tap thinking as well as recall. For example, in districts where banks of multiple-choice test items are used for benchmarking, if such items are not in the bank, then student thinking will not be part of the benchmark information. This book shows how to write both test items and performance assessments that tap higher-order thinking.

I have chosen each example to illustrate assessment of the particular aspect of higher-order thinking discussed in the various sections of the book. Because this is a book for K–12 teachers in all subjects, I have tried to select examples from a variety of subjects and grade levels. I encourage readers *not* to think, "This assessment is a good example," but rather, "What kind of thinking is this assessment a good example of?"

1 | General Principles for Assessing Higher-Order Thinking

Constructing an assessment always involves these basic principles:

- Specify clearly and exactly what it is you want to assess.
- Design tasks or test items that require students to demonstrate this knowledge or skill.
- Decide what you will take as evidence of the degree to which students have shown this knowledge or skill.

This general three-part process applies to all assessment, including assessment of higher-order thinking. Assessing higher-order thinking almost always involves three additional principles:

- Present something for students to think *about*, usually in the form of introductory text, visuals, scenarios, resource material, or problems of some sort.
- Use novel material—material that is new to the student, not covered in class and thus subject to recall.
- Distinguish between level of difficulty (easy versus hard) and level of thinking (lower-order thinking or recall versus higher-order thinking), and control for each separately.

The first part of this chapter briefly describes the general principles that apply to all assessment, because without those, assessment of anything, including higher-order thinking, fails. The second section expands on the three principles for assessing higher-order thinking. A third section deals with interpreting student responses when assessing higher-order thinking. Whether you are interpreting work for formative feedback and student improvement or scoring work for grading, you should look for qualities in the work that are signs of appropriate thinking.

Basic Assessment Principles

Begin by specifying clearly and exactly the kind of thinking, about what content, you wish to see evidence for. Check each learning goal you intend to assess to make sure that it specifies the relevant content clearly, and that it specifies what type of performance or task the student will be able to do with this content. If these are less than crystal clear, you have some clarifying to do.

This is more important than some teachers realize. It may seem like fussing with wording. After all, what's the difference between "the student understands what slope is" and "the student can solve multistep problems that involve identifying and calculating slope"? It's not just that one is wordier than the other. The second one specifies what students are able to do, specifically, that is both the target for learning and the way you will organize your assessment evidence.

If your target is just a topic, and you share it with students in a statement like "This week we're going to study slope," you are operating with the first kind of goal ("the student understands what slope is"). Arguably, one assessment method would be for you to ask students at the end of the week, "Do you understand slope now?" And, of course, they would all say, "Yes, we do."

Even with a less cynical approach, suppose you were going to give an end-of-week assessment to see what students knew about slope. What would you put on it? How would you know whether to write test items or performance tasks? One teacher might put together a test with 20 questions asking students to calculate slope using the point-slope formula. Another teacher might ask students to come up with their own problem situation in which finding the slope of a line is a major part of the solution, write it up as a small project, and include a class demonstration. These divergent approaches would probably result in different appraisals of students' achievement. Which teacher has evidence that the goal was met? As you have figured out by now, I hope, the point here is that you can't tell, because the target wasn't specified clearly enough.

Even with the better, clearer target—"The student can solve multistep problems that involve identifying and calculating slope"—you still have a target that's clear to only the teacher. Students are the ones who have to aim their thinking and their work toward the target. Before studying slope, most students would not know what a "multistep problem that involves identifying and calculating slope" looks like. To really have a clear target, you need to describe the nature of the achievement clearly for students, so they can aim for it.

In this case you might start with some examples of the kinds of problems that require knowing the rate of increase or decrease of some value with respect to the range of some other value. For example, suppose some physicians wanted to know whether and at what rate the expected life span for U.S. residents has changed since 1900. What data would they need? What would the math look like? Show students a few examples and ask them to come up with other scenarios of the same type until everyone is clear what kinds of thinking they should be able to do once they learn about slope.

Design performance tasks or test items that require students to use the targeted thinking and content knowledge. The next step is making sure the assessment really does call forth from students the desired knowledge and thinking skills. This requires that individual items and tasks tap intended learning, and that together as a set, the items or tasks on the assessment represent the whole domain of desired knowledge and thinking skills in a reasonable way.

Here's a simple example of an assessment item that does *not* tap intended learning. A teacher's unit on poetry stated the goal that students would be able to interpret poems. Her assessment consisted of a section of questions matching poems with their authors, a section requiring the identification of rhyme and meter schemes in selected excerpts from poems, and a section asking students to write an original poem. She saw these sections, rightly, as respectively tapping the new Bloom's taxonomy levels of Remember, Apply, and Create in the content area (poetry), and thought her assessment was a good one that included higher-order thinking. It is true that higher-order thinking was required. However, if you think about it, none of these items or tasks directly tapped students' ability to interpret poems.

Plan the balance of content and thinking with an assessment blueprint. Some sort of planning tool is needed to ensure that a set of assessment items or tasks represents the breadth and depth of knowledge and skills intended in your learning target or targets. The most common tool for this is an assessment blueprint. An assessment blueprint is simply a plan that indicates the balance of content knowledge and thinking skills covered by a set of assessment items or tasks. A blueprint allows your assessment to achieve the desired emphasis and balance among aspects of content and among levels of thinking. Figure 1.1 shows a blueprint for a high school history assessment on the English colonies.

The first column (Content Outline) lists the major topics the assessment will cover. The outline can be as simple or as detailed as you need to describe the content domain for your learning goals. The column headings across the top list the classifications in the Cognitive domain of the revised Bloom's taxonomy. Any other taxonomy of thinking (see Chapter 2) could be used as well.

The cells in the blueprint can list the specific learning targets and the points allocated for each, as this one does, or simply indicate the number of points allocated, depending on how comprehensive the content outline is. You can also use simpler blueprints, for example, a content-by-cognitive-level matrix without the learning targets listed. The points you select for each cell should reflect your learning target and your instruction. The example in Figure 1.1 shows a 100-point assessment to make the math easy. Each time you do your own blueprint, use the intended total points for that test as the basis for figuring percents; it will not often be exactly 100 points.

Notice that the blueprint allows you to fully describe the composition and emphasis of the assessment as a whole, so you can interpret it accurately. You can also use the blueprint to identify places where you need to add material. It is not necessary for every cell to be filled. The important thing is that the cells that are filled reflect your learning goals. Note also that the points in each cell do not all have to be 1-point test items. For example, the 10 points in the cell for

Figure 1.1 ✳ Blueprint for a High School Assessment on the English Colonies, 1607–1750

CONTENT OUTLINE	REMEMBER	UNDERSTAND	APPLY	ANALYZE	EVALUATE	CREATE
Founding of English colonies	Identify names, dates, and events.					
10 points, 10%	**10 points, 100%**					
Government of English colonies	Define proprietary, royal, and self-governing.	Describe the function of governors and legislatures in each colony.			Explain how the governments of the colonies effectively foreshadowed and prepared colonists for the American Revolution.	
25 points, 25%	**5 points, 20%**	**10 points, 40%**			**10 points, 40%**	
Life in English colonies		Describe the roles of religion, work, climate, and location in colonial life.				
15 points, 15%		**15 points, 100%**				

continued

Figure 1.1 ✳ Blueprint for a High School Assessment on the English Colonies, 1607–1750

CONTENT OUTLINE	REMEMBER	UNDERSTAND	APPLY	ANALYZE	ANALYZE	CREATE
Relations with Native Americans	Identify names, dates, and events.			Explain how colonial relations with Native Americans were influenced by land, food and resources, political events, and the French.		
25 points, 25%	5 points, 20%			20 points, 80%		
Trade, commerce, and navigation	Identify goods and resources produced in the colonies. Define the mercantile theory of trade.	Describe British trade and navigation acts. Describe the triangular trade, including its role in slavery.			Explain how salutary neglect benefited all parties involved.	
25 points, 25%	5 points, 20%	5 points, 20%			15 points, 60%	
TOTAL 100 points, 100%	25 points, 25%	30 points, 30%		20 points, 20%	25 points, 25%	

explaining how colonial governments helped prepare citizens for participation in the American Revolution could be one 10-point essay, two 5-point essays, or any combination that totals 10 points.

A blueprint helps ensure that your assessment and the information about student achievement that comes from it have the emphasis you intend. In the assessment diagrammed in Figure 1.1, three topic areas (government, relations with Native Americans, and trade—25 percent each) have more weight than colonial life (15 percent) or the founding of the colonies (10 percent). You can plan what percentage of each topic area is allocated to what level of thinking from the points and percentages within the rows. And the total at the bottom tells you the distribution of kinds of thinking across the whole assessment. In Figure 1.1, 55 percent of the assessment is allocated to recall and comprehension (25 percent plus 30 percent), and 45 percent is allocated to higher-order thinking (20 percent plus 25 percent). If the emphases don't come out the way you intend, it's a lot easier to change the values in the cells at the planning stage than to rewrite parts of the assessment later on.

In fact, blueprints simplify the task of writing an assessment. The blueprint tells you exactly what kind of tasks and items you need. You might, when seeing a blueprint like this, decide that you would rather remove one of the higher-order thinking objectives and use a project, paper, or other performance assessment for that portion of your learning goals for the unit, and a test to cover the rest of the learning goals. So, for example, you might split off the question in the cell Analyze/Native Americans and assign a paper or project for that. You could recalculate the test emphases to reflect an 80-point test, and combine the project score with the test score for the final grade for the unit.

Plan the balance of content and thinking for units. You can also use this blueprint approach for planning sets of assessments (in a unit, for example). Cross all the content for a unit with cognitive levels, then use the cells to plan how all the assessments fit together. Information about student knowledge, skills, and thinking from both tests and performance assessments can then be balanced across the unit.

Plan the balance of content and thinking for rubrics. And while we're on the subject of balance, use blueprint-style thinking to examine any rubrics you use.

Decide on the balance of points you want for each criterion, taking into account the cognitive level required for each, and make sure the whole that they create does indeed reflect your intentions for teaching, learning, and assessing. For example, a common rubric format for written projects in many subjects assesses *content completeness and accuracy*, *organization/communication*, and *writing conventions*. If each criterion is weighted equally, only one-third of the project's score reflects content. Evaluating such a rubric for balance might lead you to decide to weight the content criterion double. Or it might lead you to decide there was too much emphasis on facts and not enough on interpretation, and you might change the criteria to *content completeness and accuracy*, *soundness of thesis and reasoning*, and *writing conventions*. You might then weight the first two criteria double, leading to a score that reflects 80 percent content (40 percent each for factual information and for higher-order thinking) and 20 percent writing.

Decide what you will take as evidence that the student has, in fact, exhibited this kind of thinking about the appropriate content. After students have responded to your assessments, then what? You need a plan for interpreting their work as evidence of the specific learning you intended. If your assessment was formative (that is, it was for learning, not for grading), then you need to know how to interpret student responses and give feedback. The criteria you use as the basis for giving students feedback should reflect that clear learning target and vision of good work that you shared with the students.

If your assessment was summative (for grading), then you need to design a scheme to score student responses in such a way that the scores reflect degrees of achievement in a meaningful way. We will return to the matter of interpreting or scoring student work after we present some specific principles for assessing higher-order thinking. It will be easier to describe how to interpret or score work once we have more completely described how to prepare the tasks that will elicit that work.

Principles for Assessing Higher-Order Thinking

Put yourself in the position of a student attempting to answer a test question or do a performance assessment task. Asking "How would I (the student) have to think to answer this question or do this task?" should help you figure out what thinking skills are required for an assessment task. Asking "What would I (the student) have to think *about* to answer the question or do the task?" should help you figure out what content knowledge is required for an assessment task. As for any assessment, both should match the knowledge and skills the assessment is intended to tap. This book focuses on the first question, the question about student thinking, but it is worth mentioning that both are important and must be considered together in assessment design.

As the beginning of this chapter foreshadowed, using three principles when you write assessment items or tasks will help ensure you assess higher-order thinking: (1) use introductory material or allow access to resource material, (2) use novel material, and (3) attend separately to cognitive complexity and difficulty. In the next sections, each of these principles is discussed in more detail.

Use introductory material. Using introductory material—or allowing students to use resource materials—gives students something to think *about*. For example, student performance on a test question about *Moby Dick* that does not allow students to refer to the book might say more about whether students can recall details from *Moby Dick* than how they can think about them.

You can use introductory material with many different types of test items and performance assessment tasks. Context-dependent multiple-choice item sets, sometimes called interpretive exercises, offer introductory material and then one or several multiple-choice items based on the material. Constructed-response (essay) questions with introductory material are similar, except students must write their own answers to the questions. Performance assessments —including various kinds of papers and projects—require students to make or do something more extended than answering a test question, and can assess higher-order thinking, especially if they ask students to support their choices or thesis, explain their reasoning, or show their work. In this book, we will look at examples of each of these three assessment types.

Use novel material. Novel material means material students have not worked with already as part of classroom instruction. Using novel material means students have to actually think, not merely recall material covered in class. For example, a seemingly higher-order-thinking essay question about how Herman Melville used the white whale as a symbol is merely recall if there was a class discussion on the question "What does the white whale symbolize in *Moby Dick*?" From the students' perspective, that essay question becomes "Summarize what we said in class last Thursday."

This principle about novel material can cause problems for classroom teachers in regard to higher-order thinking. For one thing, it means that only the teacher knows for sure whether a test item or performance assessment actually assesses higher-order thinking; others outside a given classroom can't tell by looking whether or not an assessment requires higher-order thinking for that particular class. For another, the novelty of the material on an assessment is under a teacher's control. Teachers who "teach to a test" by familiarizing the students with test material intended to be novel change the nature of the assessment. However well-intentioned, this practice short-circuits the intent of the instrument to assess higher-order thinking.

Teachers should avoid short-circuiting assessments that are meant to evaluate higher-order thinking by using in class the same questions or ideas that they know will be on the test. Sometimes this is easier said than done, as students may complain—and rightly so—"we never did that before." Students should be assessed on things they were taught to do, not surprised on a test or performance assessment with tasks for which they have had no practice.

The solution is that teachers who want their students to be able to demonstrate higher-order thinking should teach it. Dealing with novel ideas, solving problems, and thinking critically should not be something students feel they "never did before." By the time students arrive at a summative assessment that requires higher-order thinking in the content domain of instruction, they should have had many opportunities to learn and practice, using other novel material.

The following example includes three versions of an assessment requiring students to discuss a theme, in this case the moral of an Aesop's fable: a multiple-choice question, an essay question, and a performance assessment. All three of the examples present the students with introductory, novel material. In this case, the material is Aesop's fable "Androcles and the Lion." Giving students the fable text means they don't need to have memorized the tale. Using a new (to them) fable means students can't rely on a previous discussion or summary of the tale. To save space, the fable is printed only once here, but it would be printed above whichever format of the question you used. You would not use all three formats, just the one most appropriate for your assessment purposes.

Androcles and the Lion

Once upon a time, a slave escaped from his master. The slave's name was Androcles. He ran into the forest and came upon a lion in distress. The lion was lying down, moaning in pain. Androcles started to run away, but the lion did not run after him. Thinking that strange, Androcles turned back. As he approached the lion, the great beast put out his paw. Androcles saw that the paw was swollen and bleeding from a huge thorn that had become embedded in it. Androcles pulled out the thorn and bandaged the lion's paw. Soon the lion was able to stand, and licked Androcles' hand like a dog. The lion took Androcles to his cave, where Androcles could hide from his master, and brought him meat to eat each day. All was well until both Androcles and the lion were captured. Androcles was sentenced to be thrown to the lion, who had not been fed for several days, as an entertainment in the arena. Many people, including the emperor, came to see the spectacle. The lion was uncaged and, eagerly anticipating a meal, charged into the arena, where Androcles was waiting. When the lion approached Androcles, however, he recognized his old friend and once again licked Androcles's hand like a dog. The emperor was surprised, summoned Androcles, and asked how this could be so. Androcles told the emperor about coming upon the lion in the forest, caring for his paw, and living in his cave. Upon hearing the tale, the emperor pardoned Androcles and freed both Androcles and the lion.

Multiple-choice question to assess reasoning about the theme

1. The theme of Aesop's fable "Androcles and the Lion" can be expressed as "Gratitude is the sign of noble souls." Choose the plot detail that best expresses the theme.

continued

A. The emperor ordered Androcles to be thrown to the lion.

*B. The lion did not eat Androcles.

C. Androcles pulled the thorn from the lion's paw.

Brief essay question to assess reasoning about the theme

2. The theme of Aesop's fable "Androcles and the Lion" can be expressed as "Gratitude is the sign of noble souls." Explain how the fable expresses this theme.

_____

_____

_____

_____

_____

_____

CRITERIA for feedback or rubrics:

- Appropriateness of details from the fable.
- Soundness of reasoning and clarity of explanation.

Performance assessment to assess reasoning about the theme

3. The theme of Aesop's fable "Androcles and the Lion" can be expressed as "Gratitude is the sign of noble souls." Write an original fable expressing the same theme. Then explain how the theme applies in a similar way to both "Androcles and the Lion" and your own fable.

CRITERIA for feedback or rubrics:

- Appropriateness of original fable to Androcles theme.
- Soundness of reasoning and clarity of explanation.
- Appropriateness of evidence from both fables.
- Writing conventions.

All three of the tasks call for analytical thinking. All three require that students be able to reason about the fable "Androcles and the Lion" and its theme. Note, however, that the formats are not completely interchangeable. They each tap a slightly different set of skills in addition to the core analysis required for explaining the theme. The multiple-choice version requires students to identify, from choices given, the portion of the fable's plot where a noble soul expresses gratitude. The short-essay version requires students to identify, from the text of the fable, the portion of the fable's plot where a noble soul expresses gratitude and to explain their reasoning. It also, therefore, requires students to exercise some writing skills. The performance assessment version requires students to do everything the short-essay version does, plus display synthetic or creative thinking to write an analogous fable and explain that thinking. It also requires more writing than the short-essay version. Which of these you would use would depend on exactly what you wanted to assess.

Manage cognitive complexity and difficulty separately. Realizing that level of difficulty (easy versus hard) and level of thinking (recall versus higher-order thinking) are two different qualities allows you to use higher-order-thinking questions and tasks with all learners. The misconception that recall is "easy" and higher-order thinking is "hard" leads to bad results. The two most insidious ones, in my opinion, are shortchanging young students and shortchanging low achievers of any age by offering them only recall and drill assignments because they are not "ready" to do higher-order thinking. In either case, while these students are waiting for you to think they are ready, they will also learn that school is boring. They may misbehave, they may drop out, and they certainly will not learn to think well.

Thinking tasks can be easy or hard, and so can recall-level tasks. If you doubt that, consider the examples on the following page.

	Easy	Difficult
Recall	Who is the main character in *The Cat in the Hat?*	Name all the characters in *Hamlet.*
Higher-Order Thinking	Why do you think the Cat cleaned up the house on his way out, before Mother got home?	Hamlet wrestles with a major question in his soliloquy, "O, that this too, too solid flesh would melt" in Act 1, Scene 2, Lines 131–161. What is the question in his mind, and how do you think he resolves it by the end of his soliloquy? State your interpretation of his major question and his resolution, and use evidence from the speech to support it.

Strategies for Giving Feedback or Scoring Tasks That Assess Higher-Order Thinking

There are two ways to interpret student responses to items or tasks: one is to comment on the work, and the other is to score it. For either, it is important to apply criteria about the quality of thinking exhibited in the work. In this book, I suggest criteria with each essay or performance assessment example (as shown in the example using the fable). The criteria could be either the foundation for feedback or the basis for rubrics, or both, depending on how you used the assessment. The important points are that the criteria match your learning targets, and that progress against those criteria means learning.

Formative Assessment of Higher-Order Thinking

Observing and discussing student reasoning directly can be a powerful way to assess higher-order thinking. Give students an assessment, and use it formatively. Have conversations with students about their reasoning, or give substantive written feedback. The conversations and feedback should be based on your learning target and criteria. Exactly what sort of thinking were you trying to assess? How should students interpret the quality of their thinking? What are some ways they might extend or deepen that thinking?

Here is an example from Robert Danka, an 8th grade mathematics teacher at Kittanning High School in Pennsylvania. He was familiarizing his students with the kind of open-ended math problems that might appear on the Pennsylvania System of School Assessment (PSSA) test. Open-ended PSSA items include phrases such as "Show all your work" and "Explain why you did each step." To do that, students need first to be able to identify the problem. Here is one part of one of the sample problems Robert used:

The Gomez family is taking a trip from Kittanning [Pennsylvania] to Atlanta, Georgia. The trip is 744 miles. They are leaving at 6 a.m. and would like to arrive at 6 p.m. How fast would they have to drive in order to arrive on time? Show and explain your work.

The major purpose for using this problem was to help students appraise the quality of their explanations of math problem solving, a formative purpose. These skills would help the students on the PSSA, a summative evaluation. This teacher gave students feedback on both the correctness of their answers and the quality of their explanations. Although it may seem automatic to the adults reading this chapter, identifying the problem as a distance problem that requires division is an important skill. Figure 1.2 (p. 32) reproduces two student responses for just the portion of the Gomez family trip problem I have used as an example.

Figure 1.2 ✳ **Examples of Student Work and Explanation of a Math Problem**

Response #1

Work:

$$\frac{62\ \text{mph}}{12\ \text{hours}\ \sqrt{744\ \text{miles}}}$$

12 hours   62 mph

Explanation: I counted how many hours they drove which is 12 then divided 12 into 744 to get my answer of 62 mph.

Response #2

Work:

$$d = rt \qquad \frac{744}{12} = \frac{r\ 12}{12} \qquad 62 = r$$

$$744 = \overset{\text{mph}}{62} \cdot \overset{\text{hours}}{12}$$

d   r   t
i   a   i
s   t   m
t   e   e
a
n
c
e

Explanation: In order to get the rate, I took the amount of hours and cancelled it out by dividing 12 by 12 and 744 by 12 and got the rate which is 62.

For Student 1, Robert wrote, "This is correct, but explain why you divided—what are you looking to find? Your explanations are improving—continue to include every piece of data in the explanation." He noticed and named one strategy (including data in the explanation) that the student had been working on and did successfully, and gave one suggestion for improvement (provide a rationale for using division). Both of these would help the student make his reasoning more transparent to a reader, and would also help with the state test expectations for explaining reasoning.

For Student 2, this teacher wrote next to $d = rt$, "Good use of the formula!" Next to the explanation, he wrote, "62__? Please refer to the question to display the units! Good explanation!" He noticed and named one specific strength (use of the formula) and made one general comment (good explanation) and one specific suggestion for improvement (specify the units).

Summative Assessment of Higher-Order Thinking

A complex task requiring higher-order thinking can be subverted by a scoring scheme that gives points only for facts reported. Conversely, scoring the quality of students' reasoning on even some very simple tasks can assess higher-order thinking. For summative assessment of how students use higher-order thinking—for graded tests and projects—a scoring scheme must be devised in such a way that higher-order thinking is required to score well. This requirement means that soundness of thinking must figure into the criteria from which the rubric is developed. Some rubrics or other scoring schemes attend mainly to surface features or merely count the number of correct facts in students' responses. Such scoring schemes can turn an exercise in which students *did use* higher-order thinking into a score that *doesn't reflect* the thinking students did.

Multiple-choice questions. Multiple-choice questions would typically be scored with one point for a correct choice and no points for an incorrect choice. The "thinking" is encoded into the choosing. It is worth reminding readers here that for the resulting scores to mean that students use higher-order thinking, the questions have to be designed so that higher-order thinking really is required to answer.

Constructed-response and essay questions. For constructed-response answers to questions designed to tap various kinds of reasoning, often a rubric with a short scale will work well. Start with the criterion, the type of thinking you intended to assess. For example, ask, "Does the student weigh evidence before making decisions?" or "Does the student appropriately evaluate the credibility of the source?" Then use a scale that gives partial credit depending on the quality of the reasoning.

Here is an example of a task a 9th grade science teacher used to assess students' understanding of chemical and physical changes. Students had observed demonstrations about ice floating in water, then melting, and had drawn diagrams of the molecular structure. Then pairs of students were given cards with everyday events. They were to sort them into two categories, physical change and chemical change, and explain why they put them where they did. Then they were to write what they learned about physical and chemical changes. In passing, I should mention that this exercise sparked some interesting student higher-order thinking beyond simple categorizing and inductive thinking. For example, one student asked, "Is cutting the grass a chemical or physical change, if you consider that the cut part of the grass dies?"

Here is an example of a scoring scheme that could be used with the 9th grade science class example of physical and chemical changes. I list the scale as 2-1-0, but it could also be 3-2-1, or 6-4-2, or whatever weight is appropriate for other scores with which it needs to be combined for a particular test or grade composite score.

Did the student reason inductively from the examples to arrive at a clear, accurate description of physical and chemical changes?

2 = Completely and clearly—Response gives clear evidence of reasoning from the examples.

1 = Partially—Response is accurate, but reasoning from examples isn't clear or is only partial.

0 = No—Response does not demonstrate reasonable conclusions from the examples.

Figure 1.3 presents responses from three student pairs. Each pair was to list one example of physical and chemical change, and then a paragraph explaining what the pair had learned about physical and chemical changes from their inductive reasoning. Response 1 would score a 0. The teacher did not think that these students showed any evidence of having figured out differences between physical and chemical changes based on sorting the examples. Response 2 would score a 1. These students' statement about molecular structure is correct, but as the teacher commented, "Textbook response, got the concept but I'm not sure if it was from discussion." The response does not allow us to conclude much about their reasoning. Response 3 would score a 2. In fact, the teacher was very pleased and said, "Not an answer I would expect, but they really got the concept."

Figure 1.3 ✳ **Examples of Student Explanations of Physical and Chemical Changes**

Response #1   **Score: 0**

Physical: Ripping paper   Chemical: Burning paper

I've learned that during physical changes and chemical changes there can be alot of arguements and disputes. Also physical changes can be very difficult to recognize. Chemical changes are basically just common sense.

Response #2   **Score: 1**

Physical: Cutting a banana   Chemical: Baking soda & vinegar

Chemical changes occur when there is a change in the molecular structure of an object. Physical however the shape or form changes while molecular structure stays the same.

Response #3   **Score: 2**

Physical: Cleaning your locker   Chemical: Melting plastic

I learned that you can not base the type of change on the object. Just because it may look like a physical doesn't mean it is. You have to figure out that if you can get it back the way it was, if not then its chemical.

Performance assessments. Analytical rubrics are often used for scoring performance assessments, papers, and projects. The quality of thinking demonstrated in the work should figure prominently in at least one of the rubric trait scales.

Teachers can write their own rubrics or select a rubric for use from among the many that are available on the Internet or in curriculum materials. An Internet search for "problem-solving rubrics," for example, yielded 85,500 results.

Before you use rubrics from the Internet or from curriculum materials, make sure they are good ones that will help you communicate clearly. Select or write rubrics that are appropriate to the content and thinking skills you intend to assess and that are appropriate for the educational development of your students. Select or write rubrics that describe qualities (e.g., "reasoning is logical and thoughtful") rather than count things (e.g., "includes at least three reasons").

It is particularly helpful if the same general thinking or problem-solving scheme can be applied to several different assignments. Students will learn that the thinking and reasoning qualities described in the rubric are their "learning target" and can practice generalizing them across the different assignments. The general rubrics can be used with each assignment or can be made specific for that assignment.

Excellent examples of problem-solving rubrics for different purposes exist, and many are available on the Internet. The NWREL Mathematics Problem-Solving Scoring Guide uses five criteria: *conceptual understanding, strategies and reasoning, computation and execution, communication*, and *insights*. Descriptions of performance on each criterion are given for each of four levels: *emerging, developing, proficient*, and *exemplary*. The rubric is available online at http://educationnorthwest.org/content/851.

In 2008, the School-wide Rubrics Committee at Lincoln High School in Lincoln, Rhode Island, developed several rubrics for teachers and students to use, many based on the National English Language Arts Standards. One of the schoolwide rubrics is for problem solving and is available online at www.lincolnps.org/HighSchool/rubrics/Problem-Solving%20School-wide%20Rubric.pdf. This rubric describes five criteria: *understands the problem and devises a plan, implements a plan, reflects on results, creates an organizing structure*, and *demonstrates understanding of written language conventions (when appropriate)*. The rubric describes performance at each of four levels: *exceeds standard, meets standard, nearly meets standard*, and *below standard*.

The state of Kentucky uses an open-ended scoring guide for problem solving in mathematics, social studies, science, and arts and humanities. This general rubric can be defined in more specific detail for specific assessment items or tasks. The advantage of using such a general framework as the basis for scoring all kinds of work is that students will come to see the types of thinking expected in the general rubric as learning goals. They will be able to practice and work consistently toward these achievement outcomes. This rubric is holistic, which means it uses one overall scale to rate performance. It is called the Kentucky General Scoring Guide and is contained in each booklet of released items for the Kentucky Core Content Test (KCCT). Links to released items at different content areas and grade levels are available online at www. education.ky.gov/KDE/Administrative+Resources/Testing+and+Reporting+/ District+Support/Link+to+Released+Items/2009+KCCT+Released+Items.htm.

There are many more excellent rubrics to be found. Use your own evaluative skills when searching for and appraising rubrics for your own purposes. When you select rubrics to use or to adapt for use, make sure that the criteria (scoring categories or traits) match the problem-solving or other skills you value and teach. Make sure that the descriptions of quality in each of the levels (*proficient*, and so on) match the expectations for performance in your school and district. Use rubrics not only for scoring summative assessments, but for instruction and formative assessment as well. For example, students can use rubrics to analyze the qualities of work samples, to self-assess drafts of their own work, to discuss work with peers, or to form the basis of student-teacher conferences.

Summing Up

This chapter discussed three general assessment principles, three specific principles for assessing higher-order thinking, and ways to interpret or score the student work from such assessments. I think of the material in this chapter as "the basics." These principles underlie all the assessment examples in the rest of the book. As you read the more specific examples in the following chapters, think of how each one works out these basic principles in the specific instance.

This should help you develop the skills to apply these principles when you write your own assessments.

2 | Assessing Analysis, Evaluation, and Creation

Teaching for transfer, or teaching for meaning, involves enabling students not only to remember and understand but also to use knowledge in increasingly more complex ways (Anderson & Krathwohl, 2001). A taxonomy can help you bring to mind the wide range of important learning targets and thinking skills you want students to attain. For any content domain, you typically want students to know some facts and concepts and also to be able to think and reason with these facts and concepts in some way. Each time students solve new problems or do original thinking with their knowledge, they are transferring and transforming what they learned, and their understanding grows.

Bloom's is probably the most commonly used taxonomy in the United States, but there are other taxonomies, too. They are all useful for categorizing learning objectives and assessments according to level of complexity: from recall through near transfer (applying ideas in a manner similar to how they were taught) and through far transfer (using ideas in farther-ranging and more complex contexts than originally taught). Your instruction and assessment should match your intended learning target in both content (what the student learns) and cognitive complexity (what the student is able to do with the learning).

What Are Cognitive Taxonomies?

Cognitive taxonomies are organized schemes for classifying instructional learning targets into various levels of complexity. Several different taxonomies have been developed for sorting learning targets.

The *Taxonomy of Educational Objectives, Handbook I: Cognitive Domain* (Bloom, Engelhart, Furst, Hill, & Krathwohl, 1956) is the taxonomy many readers may have studied during their teacher education programs. Despite its age, Bloom's taxonomy is still used in many curriculum and teaching materials. The taxonomy classifies cognitive performances into six major headings arranged from simple to complex:

1. **Knowledge** involves the recall of facts and concepts.
2. **Comprehension** involves basic understanding. The classic assessment to see whether students comprehend a concept or story is to ask them to restate it in their own words.
3. **Application** involves using facts and concepts to solve new or novel problems, but they can be problems that are similar to ones students have solved before. Application-level problems usually have one correct answer.
4. **Analysis** involves breaking down information into its parts and then reasoning with that information. There are often many different acceptable responses to analysis-level tasks.
5. **Synthesis** involves putting parts together to form a new whole. Synthesis-level tasks require arranging ideas in a new or original way.
6. **Evaluation** involves judging the value of materials and methods for various purposes. Evaluation-level activities usually ask students to make a claim about the worth of something and explain their reasons.

Anderson and Krathwohl and a group of colleagues published a revision of the Bloom *handbook* in 2001. A major difference between the revised taxonomy and the original is that the 2001 version has two dimensions—Knowledge and Cognitive Process. The Knowledge dimension classifies the kind of knowledge a student deals with: facts, concepts, procedures, or metacognition. The Cognitive Process dimension looks very much like the original Bloom's taxonomy except that the order of the last two categories is reversed. Because the

Knowledge dimension uses the word *knowledge*, the first level of the Cognitive dimension is called "Remember." So we have the following:

1. **Remember** involves recognizing or recalling facts and concepts.

2. **Understand** involves basic comprehension, understood in light of newer theories of learning that emphasize students constructing their own meaning. Processes in this category include interpreting, exemplifying, classifying, summarizing, inferring, comparing, and explaining.

3. **Apply** means to execute or implement a procedure to solve a problem. Application-level problems still usually have one best answer.

4. **Analyze** means to break information into its parts, determining how the parts are related to each other and to the overall whole. Processes include differentiating, organizing, and attributing. Multiple correct responses are still likely in analysis-level tasks.

5. **Evaluate** means judging the value of material and methods for given purposes, based on criteria. Processes include checking and critiquing.

6. **Create** means putting disparate elements together to form a new whole, or reorganizing existing elements to form a new structure. Processes include generating, planning, and producing.

There are other taxonomies. Assessment standards for the Dimensions of Learning model (Marzano, Pickering, & McTighe, 1993) distinguish Declarative Knowledge, Procedural Knowledge, Complex Thinking, Information Processing, Effective Communication, Cooperation, and Habits of Mind. Each of the last five categories includes descriptions of various thinking processes that could be considered higher-order thinking.

More recently, Marzano and Kendall (2007), like Anderson and Krathwohl (2001), have distinguished knowledge from types of thinking. Marzano and Kendall identify three domains of knowledge: Information, Mental Procedures, and Psychomotor Procedures. Their Systems of Thinking form a hierarchy of levels of processing: (1) Retrieval, (2) Comprehension, (3) Analysis, (4) Knowledge Utilization, (5) Metacognition, and (6) Self-System Thinking.

The cognitive demands of many state accountability tests are analyzed with Webb's (2002) Depth of Knowledge levels. Webb uses four levels to classify the

level of thinking required to do various cognitive activities: (1) Recall and Repro-
duction, (2) Skill and Concept, (3) Strategic Thinking, and (4) Extended Thinking.

Another cognitive taxonomy, widely used in Australia, New Zealand, Can-
ada, and the United Kingdom, is the SOLO Taxonomy (Biggs & Collis, 1982).
SOLO stands for Structure of Observed Learning Outcomes. It is a hierarchical
taxonomy of thinking skills that focuses on how many elements, and how many
relationships among the elements, the student needs to think about. It has five
levels: (1) Prestructural, (2) Unistructural, (3) Multistructural, (4) Relational,
and (5) Extended Abstract.

What these taxonomies of cognitive processes clearly have in common
is that as the thinking level gets more complex, students need to deal with
increasingly more pieces of information and increasingly more complicated
relationships among them. This chapter explores ways to assess higher-order
thinking conceived in that way, as the top end of a cognitive taxonomy, requiring transfer of ideas from the context in which they were taught to new contexts.

Using the new Bloom's taxonomy, we now turn to ways to assess students'
abilities to analyze, evaluate, and create. You will notice that these assessments
demonstrate the principles described in Chapter 1. For example, most of them
rely on presenting introductory material that is new to the student.

Assessing Analysis

To assess the quality of students' thinking as they break down information into
its parts and reason with that information, questions or tasks must ask students
to find or describe those parts and figure out how they are related. Analysis-
level questions present students with material (or ask them to locate material),
then ask questions or present problems whose answers require differentiating
or organizing the parts in some reasonable manner. Explaining the reasoning
used to relate the parts to one another is often part of the analysis task.

The examples that follow show some typical kinds of analysis-level questions in several different content areas and grade levels. This is not an exhaus-
tive list. Use your own content- and grade-level examples to extend the various
kinds of questions to fit a wide range of contexts.

Focus on a Question or Main Idea

Focusing on a question or main idea, or "getting the point" of something, is a central analytical skill in most disciplines. The Androcles examples in Chapter 1 were of this type. This ability is easiest to see in the foundational skill that elementary teachers would call identifying the main idea in text. At the analysis level, we are talking about finding the main idea in a text that doesn't state the main idea explicitly. If it does, of course, all students have to do is remember and understand it. To require analysis-level thinking, students need to infer the main idea from the individual points made in a text, taken as a whole.

I'm using "text" in the broad sense here, to mean a written text, speech, documentary, situation, set of events, and so on, that students can critically review to determine the main points, thesis, or argument. Students should be able to formulate or select appropriate criteria by which to evaluate this main point, thesis, or argument. This kind of task is "analysis" because to identify the main idea, students have to break the text into parts and see what the parts have in common and what message they point to or support. This is classic analysis—break something into parts, then see relationships among the parts.

To assess how students focus on a question, give students a statement of a problem or policy, a political address or cartoon, or an experiment and results. Then ask students what the main issue or problem is. You could also ask what criteria they would use to evaluate the quality, goodness, or truth of the argument or conclusions.

Here is a social studies example of multiple-choice questions assessing students' ability to identify the main idea in a portion of the Declaration of Independence. Notice that this set of questions follows the principles for assessing higher-order thinking. Novel material is presented, in this case a passage from the Declaration of Independence.

Questions 4 and 5 refer to the passage below from the Declaration of Independence.

> We hold these truths to be self-evident, that all men are created equal, that they are endowed by their Creator with certain

continued

unalienable Rights, that among these are Life, Liberty and the pursuit of Happiness. That to secure these rights, Governments are instituted among Men, deriving their just powers from the consent of the governed, that whenever any Form of Government becomes destructive of these ends, it is the Right of the People to alter or to abolish it, and to institute new Government, laying its foundation on such principles and organizing its powers in such form, as to them shall seem most likely to effect their Safety and Happiness.

4. According to the passage, the most important purpose of government is to protect

    A. People from harm.
    B. The church.
    C. The truth.
    *D. People's rights.

5. Which statement best summarizes the main point being made in the passage?

    *A. The people should be in control of their own government.
    B. The church should help governments determine what is right.
    C. The main function of government is to keep people happy.
    D. Governments need to be changed regularly to keep them from becoming unjust.

Source: National Assessment of Educational Progress, Civics, grade 8, Block 2006-8C4, nos. 4–5. Available: http://nces.ed.gov/nationsreportcard/itmrlsx/landing.aspx

Question 4 begins the set with a comprehension (or understanding) question. Question 4 calls for comprehension or understanding because the passage directly states: ". . . to secure these rights, Governments. . . ."

Question 5 is an example of asking students to identify the main idea. To arrive at the correct answer, students have to consider the parts of the text, including the purpose of government to secure rights, the source of government's power, and the people's right to change governments for causes related to their safety and happiness. Then the students have to reason that, taken together, these parts constitute the main idea that people should be in control of their own government. Some teachers who are reading this book may be so familiar with this principle that for them it is not analysis, just recall, to come to this conclusion. In fact, some teachers may have explicitly taught this theme to their students, and for those students this question could be at the recall level as well. However, this question is at the analysis level for students who have to extract the main point from the reading.

Notice that Question 5 is not about reasoning alone, but about reasoning with content. The main content—the excerpt from the Declaration of Independence—is supplied. Other basic content knowledge, however, is required, most notably in this case, what a government is. You need to analyze the content knowledge and reasoning requirements of a question and make sure they match what you intend the question to measure. If a question requires background or content knowledge that is not part of the intended domain, then the question should be revised. In this case, reasoning about the nature of government is exactly what is wanted.

An essay version of this assessment item could also be used. One example of how to do this follows:

[Teacher inserts the passage here.]

What is the main point of the passage above? State the main point in your own words, and then give evidence from the passage.

CRITERIA for feedback or rubrics:

- Clear, appropriate statement of the main point.
- Appropriateness of evidence.
- Soundness of reasoning and clarity of explanation.

These criteria should be the basis for feedback (with or without a score) if the assessment is used for formative purposes. These criteria could become the basis for scoring rubrics if the assessment is used for grading. A single holistic rubric could incorporate all three criteria, as in this example:

Does the student identify the main point and clearly support it with evidence from the text?

> 2 = Completely and clearly—Main point is clearly stated, and evidence from the passage supports it. Explanation is clear.

> 1 = Partially—Main point is stated, but not well supported with evidence from the passage. Explanation is not completely clear.

> 0 = No—Main point is not stated or is not correct. Evidence from the passage is missing.

Alternatively, each criterion could become the basis for one part of an analytic rubric, as in Figure 2.1, which would be used as a set (total 6 points) to score students' work.

Figure 2.1 ✳ An Analytic Rubric for Identifying the Main Idea

	2	1	0
Thesis (statement of the main point)	Thesis is clear, is complete, and accurately reflects the main point.	Thesis is clear and at least partially reflects the main point.	Thesis is not clear and/or does not reflect the main point.
Evidence	Evidence is accurate, relevant, and complete.	Evidence is mostly clear, relevant, and complete.	Evidence is not clear, relevant, or complete.
Reasoning and clarity	The way in which the evidence supports the thesis is clear, logical, and well explained.	The way in which the evidence supports the thesis is mostly clear and logical. Some explanation is given.	The way in which the evidence supports the thesis is not clear, is illogical, and/or is not explained.

Analyze Arguments or Theses

Once an author's main point, argument, or thesis is identified, it can be further analyzed. Identifying underlying assumptions, representing the logic or structure of the argument, finding irrelevancies if there are any, and judging the similarities or differences in two or more arguments are all analysis skills.

To assess how students analyze arguments, give students an argument—a text or a speech, for example. Then ask students one or more of the following questions:

- What evidence does the author give that supports the argument(s)?
- What evidence does the author give that contradicts the argument(s)?
- What assumptions need to hold for the argument(s) to be valid?
- Are any part(s) of the statement irrelevant to the argument(s)?
- What is the logical structure of the argument(s)?

I once observed a college freshman composition class in which many students struggled with an assignment to "analyze the structure of Jefferson's argument for democracy in the Declaration of Independence." Some of these students did not really grasp the concept that the Declaration of Independence *was* an argument, much less something they could analyze. They had all been taught that this document was an important event in history. Some had even memorized parts of it. Years of "recall-level" interaction with the Declaration had left some of them so stuck in lower-order thinking about it that they had trouble approaching the assignment.

Remember the caution that higher-order thinking happens only if the students do the analysis themselves. In less than a minute on the Internet, I found an analysis of the structure of the Declaration's argument in Wikipedia. Beware: a less than comprehensive, but original, analysis by a student is still an example of analysis; an elegant rendition of someone else's argument is merely evidence of comprehension.

Here is an example for high school English. This example illustrates how important it is for you to clearly define what sort of thinking you want to assess before you write the assessment task. There are so many questions you could ask about this sonnet that you would need to know for sure what kind of thinking you wanted students to do in order to figure out what to ask. The following example presents a brief performance task to assess analyzing an argument that also requires understanding the author's point of view.

Shakespeare's Sonnet 149 is an argument offered to a cruel woman who, we can infer, must have said to the author, "I don't love you." Here is the text of the sonnet:

> Canst thou, O cruel! say I love thee not,
> When I against myself with thee partake?
> Do I not think on thee, when I forgot
> Am of myself, all tyrant, for thy sake?
> Who hateth thee that I do call my friend?
> On whom frown'st thou that I do fawn upon?
> Nay, if thou lour'st on me, do I not spend
> Revenge upon myself with present moan?
> What merit do I in myself respect,
> That is so proud thy service to despise,
> When all my best doth worship thy defect,
> Commanded by the motion of thine eyes?
> But, love, hate on, for now I know thy mind;
> Those that can see thou lovest, and I am blind.

—William Shakespeare, Sonnet 149

In a brief paper, analyze the poem in two ways. In the first section, you will analyze the argument Shakespeare makes, that is, from the poet's point of view. In the second section, you will analyze the argument from your own point of view.

1. First, in your own words, state the main point in the poet's argument to the woman and explain the reasons the poet gives to support this argument. When you use evidence from the poem, cite it in Shakespeare's words and also in modern English (your own words). Explain the poet's reasoning.

2. From your point of view, is this a sound argument? Is it valid and logical, and does it make sense? Explain your own reasoning.

CRITERIA for feedback or rubrics for Question 1:

- Clear, appropriate statement of the main point.
- Appropriateness of evidence.
- Soundness of reasoning and clarity of explanation.

CRITERIA for feedback or rubrics for Question 2:

- Clear, appropriate statement of the student's own evaluation of the argument.
- Appropriateness of evidence.
- Soundness of reasoning and clarity of explanation.

This performance assessment could be a summative assessment, scored with rubrics. You could use holistic or analytic rubrics similar to those in the previous section. For Question 1, the thesis is the main point, and the rubrics work without modification. For Question 2, the thesis is the student's evaluation of the poet's argument, and you would modify the rubrics accordingly. You could use the three criteria alone or with others to assess the use of writing conventions, depending on whether written expression was part of the learning you intended to assess. If you were going to assess the writing itself, you would say so right in the directions for the tasks.

Give the students the rubrics at the same time you give them the task so they can self-assess as they do their work. You could build formative assessment opportunities into the work by planning opportunities for self-assessment, peer assessment, or teacher feedback on drafts of the work in progress.

You could also use this performance task as a practice assessment, for formative purposes. You would still give the students the rubric at the beginning, but instead of using it to score students' work for a grade, you would use it to organize written or oral feedback. This formative assessment would help prepare students to analyze the argument in a different text at the end of the unit, for grading.

Compare and Contrast

Not all "comparison and contrast" tasks require higher-order thinking. Simple comparison and contrast is one way to show understanding. For example, the question "How is a lemon like an orange?" answered with the response "They are both citrus fruit" gives evidence that a student understands what citrus fruit is. I mention this because there are many charts that link certain verbs with certain levels of thinking. "Compare" and "contrast" are two verbs that serve several different levels of thinking, and you simply have to analyze (no pun intended) what the question asks of students before you can decide what level of thinking is required.

More complex comparison and contrast questions do require analysis-level thinking. Present students with material or ask them to locate material, and then set a task that requires students to identify various elements in it and organize those elements according to whether they are alike or not alike. Comparison and contrast is an important all-purpose analysis skill and is usually taught explicitly in elementary school. Some teachers use a Venn diagram to help students organize the elements visually before they begin to write about them.

Patti McCausland, a 4th grade teacher at West Hills Intermediate Elementary School in Pennsylvania, gave her students a comparison and contrast task. She asked her students to choose two objects, identify at least four attributes of each that were alike and four that were different, use a Venn diagram, and then write an essay. The essay was to have an introductory paragraph, a paragraph about similarities, a paragraph about differences, and a final paragraph. Students were to use appropriate transition words and follow the conventions of good writing. So this teacher was using the assessment to appraise both higher-order thinking and written composition skills.

For Patti's 4th graders, student choice of material in effect became a little problem to solve, because students needed to choose things that were somewhat alike, somewhat different, and about which they knew enough to write. Then students needed to break their objects down into parts (the attributes of each that they selected to compare and contrast) and organize those parts (alike/not alike, first using the Venn diagram and then using the essay format). Let's look at two student responses to this assignment and walk through an analysis of the student thinking demonstrated in the responses.

We will set aside an analysis of the writing itself and concentrate on the *thinking*. Remember from Chapter 1 that if you want to assess student thinking, you have to look at the thinking itself. This is the case whether your feedback to the students is in the form of written comments, scores/grades, or both. Sometimes it is hard not to confound handwriting, spelling, grammar, length, and even topic in your analysis of student thinking. The best way to avoid confounding your assessment of thinking and writing is to assess the merits of each separately. This gives you a framework within which to register all of your comments. If the assessment is for grading, you can weight the two dimensions (thinking, writing) according to the emphasis in the learning goals you are assessing.

Figure 2.2 presents the work of one successful student and one less successful student. Typesetting has removed any influence handwriting might have on readers, but differences in the students' spelling, grammar, essay length, and topic are still apparent. These two are useful examples because with just a quick read, a teacher might say that Student 1's work is better than Student 2's work. However, their analyses are of similar quality.

Figure 2.2 ✳ Students' Comparison and Contrast Essays

Student #1

I'm comparing clarinets and saxaphones because I like these instruments.
Clarinets and saxaphones are alike because they both are instruments, have reeds, are hard to play. They have to be cleaned regularly.
Clarinets and saxaphones are different because, clarinets are black, but saxaphones are gold. Saxaphones are big but, clarinets are smaller. Clarinets need just some air but, saxaphones need alot. Saxaphones' reeds are bigger than clarinet reeds. Clarinets are low. Saxaphones are high.
I compared clarinets and saxaphones because I like these instruments and the sounds are cool because one is low and one is high.

Student #2

My sister and I are different like Morgan has brown hair and I have blond hair. Morgan has brown eyes and I have blue eyes, Morgan has straight hair and I have curly hair. We have different ages too Morgan is twelve years old. and I am ten years old.
We are alike in ways too like We are smart, We are tall, We are both funny, and we like the same stores.
I chose my sister and I because we are alike and different in many different ways.

Student 1 clearly understands the concepts of comparison and contrast, and applies them to clarinets and saxophones. Four similarities are listed correctly: they are instruments, have reeds, are hard to play, and need to be cleaned. Five differences are listed—color, size of instrument, amount of air required, size of reed, and pitch—but one is not correct. Based on the information about size and color, the student is probably thinking of an alto or a tenor saxophone, and if so, the pitch description is backward (the saxophone would sound lower than the clarinet).

Student 2 also clearly understands the concepts of comparison and contrast, and applies them to herself and her sister. Four similarities are listed: smart, tall, funny, and favorite stores. Four differences are listed: differences in hair color, eye color, hair texture, and age.

Analyzed in this way, it appears that both students demonstrate the quality of the comparison/contrast thinking that the teacher intended. What is different in quality between the two essays is following directions (there were supposed to be four paragraphs, and similarities were supposed to come first), spelling (Student 1 misspelled *saxophone*, while Student 2 had no spelling errors but did not use difficult words), and especially grammar and usage. Student 2's essay is a poor specimen when it comes to writing conventions, and Student 1's paper is a good specimen.

Student 2 chose a personal comparison, and Student 1 chose a more academic comparison, between two band instruments. Although Student 1's is a more academically sophisticated choice, the teacher did allow students to choose freely.

Bottom line: be careful how you read student papers. Analyze the thinking and writing separately. Then you will be able to give more targeted and helpful feedback. Student 2 needs to work on her writing, and she also needs to know that she *does* understand how to use comparison and contrast. Without separate feedback for thinking and writing, the student could misunderstand a mediocre grade for this work to mean her thinking was faulty.

Assessing Evaluation

To assess evaluation, you need items or tasks that can assess how students judge the value of materials and methods for their intended purposes. Students can appraise the material against criteria. The criteria can be standard (for example, literary, historical, scientific) or criteria that the students invent themselves (in which case an element of creativity is involved as well). This kind of evaluation isn't a personal preference ("Chocolate is the best flavor of ice cream"), but a reasoned evaluation that can be stated as a thesis or a conclusion and supported with evidence and logic. To assess how well students can do evaluation, give them some material and ask them to judge its value for some purpose.

Questions requiring literary criticism are an example of this type of evaluation. Literary criticism answers questions such as these: How effectively did the author use imagery? How compellingly did a situation grab a reader's attention or elicit an emotional response? In fact, most critiques of anything—art or music reviews or critiques, restaurant reviews, book reviews—are evaluations. In both the natural and social sciences, reviews of literature that appraise how strong the evidence is for supporting a theory (for instance, the big bang theory of the birth of the universe) are evaluations. A good current example of the importance of evaluation as a thinking skill are the reviews and articles appearing in both the scientific and popular press evaluating the evidence about global warming.

An "old standby" assignment, the 4th grade two-paragraph book report, is a good example of assessing evaluative thinking. Do you remember assignments like these from your elementary school days, as I do? The assignments I remember were to read a book, then write a two-paragraph book report. In the first paragraph, summarize what the book was about (this is thinking at the Understand level). In the second paragraph, tell what was your favorite part, and why. This second paragraph should require thinking at the Evaluate level. The student must present a thesis ("The part I liked best was . . .") and support it with evidence. The teacher should be more interested in how well the thesis was supported—whether the evidence from the book was accurate, relevant, and logically explained—than in what part was the student's favorite.

In the following example, an elementary science teacher wants to assess how well her students understand the concept of "control" in experimental design:

In Maya's science class, the teacher wanted students to design experiments to find out about temperature changes. Each student was to plan and conduct a simple experiment, measure and graph temperature changes, and write a report about the findings. Maya decided she wanted to study how long it takes coffee to cool. Her teacher said she would bring a coffeemaker to class. Here are Maya's plans for the experiment.

Maya's Plan
I'm going to ask my teacher to make the coffee. I'll put it in a cup, and I'll measure its temperature with a thermometer, every five minutes for an hour. I'll make a line graph of the temperature. I should be able to see how fast the line drops as the coffee gets cooler.

Do you think Maya's plan is a good one? Why or why not? Would you suggest any changes to her plan? If so, tell what you would change and explain why.

CRITERIA for feedback or rubrics:

- Clear, appropriate statement(s) evaluating Maya's experiment.
- Appropriateness of evidence.
- Soundness of scientific reasoning and clarity of explanation.

In this experimental plan, several things relevant to the speed of coffee cooling are not controlled: coffee temperature before cooling, air temperature, volume of coffee, kind of cup (foam, china, plastic, and so on). You would assess students' evaluation of the experimental plan and suggestions for improvement according to how well they identified these uncontrolled aspects and how appropriately they explained why each needed to be controlled. A rubric, feedback, or both could be used, depending on the purpose of your assessment. A holistic rubric based on these criteria might look like the following:

Does the student's evaluation identify uncontrolled aspects of the experiment and explain why they need to be controlled?

2 = Completely and clearly—Uncontrolled aspects of the experiment are clearly identified and evaluated as inadequate. Reasoning is explained and is related to the concept of experimental control. Explanation is clear.

1 = Partially—Some uncontrolled aspects of the experiment are identified and evaluated as inadequate. Some reasoning may not be clearly explained or not entirely related to the concept of experimental control.

0 = No—Uncontrolled aspects of the experiment are not identified, or no evaluation is given. Reasoning is missing or not related to the concept of experimental control. Explanation is not clear.

Note that this is a task-specific rubric and could not be shared with students before the assessment. Students should be told, however, that they will be assessed on their evaluation of the quality of the experimental plan, their reasoning and use of evidence, and clarity of explanation.

Assessing Creation

To assess whether students can "create" in the Bloom's taxonomy sense means assessing whether they can put unlike things together in a new way, or reorganize existing things to make something new. Present students with a task to do or a problem to solve that includes generating multiple solutions, planning a procedure to accomplish a particular goal, or producing something new. The creation we are discussing here is what the old Bloom's taxonomy called "synthesis," and it overlaps with creativity in the broader sense. Here I give some examples of assessing synthetic, creative thinking about academic problems. See Chapter 6 for more about assessment of creativity and creative thinking.

A language arts assignment that asks students to write an original ending to a story can assess whether students can reorganize existing things (in this case, story elements like plot, characters, and setting) to make something new. There would be multiple ways to do that, but it's not "anything goes." Only alternative endings that fit with the story's plot, characters, and setting would be good endings. In science, an original experiment to test a particular hypothesis requires creating an experimental design. In any subject, planning a research paper—deciding on a research question, a method for obtaining information, and a plan for synthesizing it into a paper—requires creation. In mathematics, writing original story problems for particular number sentences or equations requires creation. All of these examples are performance assessments that could be scored with rubrics or given feedback with or without scoring.

I once observed a 5th grade class where students were studying colonial America and events leading up to the American Revolution. In groups of four, they wrote skits. Each skit needed to have four characters from the period (one for each student to perform), and the dialogue they wrote had to be appropriate to the role of each character. For example, a British soldier would have lines expressing loyalty to King George III, an American farmer might have lines expressing "no taxation without representation," a Native American might have lines describing encroachment on native land, and so on. One of the things that impressed me with this observation was that the teacher resisted the opportunity to go for the "cute factor." She looked beyond colorful costumes and hammy acting, which provided great fun for all, and graded the students on the content of their thinking and the clarity of their expression of ideas. This performance assessment provided a vehicle for the teacher to assess her students' ability to reason creatively with the information they were studying.

Formative and Summative Uses of Results

The goal of using a cognitive taxonomy is to help students transfer their knowledge to new situations. The purpose of assessment of analysis, evaluation, or creation is to get information about the ways in which students use their knowledge and skills in novel situations.

Any of the three formats—multiple-choice questions, constructed-response or essay questions, and performance assessment—can be used formatively for learning, or summatively for grading. The methods of constructing the assessments are the same for both purposes. What is different is how the results are presented and used.

For formative assessment, students as well as teachers need to understand what assessment results tell them about their thinking. The multiple-choice questions about the Declaration of Independence could be used, for example, with classroom-response systems (clickers) or ABCD cards as a check on student understanding. Students could then discuss the thinking behind their choices, either in class discussion or in some kind of structured activity. The teacher could ask two students with different answer choices to explain their reasoning to each other, while the rest of the class observes "fishbowl" style, followed by discussion of what they learned.

For formative assessment, the essay questions could receive feedback in the form of comments only, receive both comments and scores, or provide input for paired discussions and revision. Longer performance assessments like the analysis of the lovelorn poet's argument to his lady in Shakespeare's Sonnet 149 could prompt feedback on outlines, drafts, and other preliminary products in time for the final performance to benefit from the feedback.

An important part of formative feedback on items or tasks requiring analysis, evaluation, or creation should be feedback on the thinking itself. Instead of concentrating solely on whether students have arrived at appropriate literary, historical, scientific, or mathematical conclusions, make sure to coach students on the soundness of their reasoning, their selection of evidence, and the clarity of their explanations. Model sound reasoning, good use of evidence, and clear explanations for students.

For summative assessment, the multiple-choice questions would be scored right or wrong, and rubrics or other scoring schemes would be used for essay questions and performance assessments. For summative (graded) assessment, students will pay more attention to the grade than to written or oral feedback comments.

The most effective planning, then, uses formative assessment of analysis, evaluation, and creation during instruction, with plenty of written and oral feedback. Focus what time and energy you have for giving feedback on this formative phase of the instructional unit. The goal is to help students adjust their thinking so that they can "show what they know" on the summative assessment. At the culmination of the unit, it makes most sense to grade the summative assessment with very few comments. Certainly comment if there is something important to say or if a student asks a question about the work, but don't take a lot of time formulating comments students won't have the opportunity to use, for learning targets for which you have already finished instruction.

Student Self-Assessment and Use of Results as a Special Case

Student self-assessment requires higher-order thinking. To participate in the formative assessment process—*Where am I going? Where am I now? What do I need to do to close the gap?*—students need to use a combination of analysis, evaluation, and creation. They need to understand various aspects of their own work (analysis), evaluate these aspects against criteria (evaluation), and figure out what the next step should be (creating a plan). An important thing to check when self-assessment is not going well is the quality of students' thinking. Are they really analyzing their work, or are they just checking the "OK" boxes on a checklist? If that's a problem, are they resisting self-assessment, or do they really need help evaluating their work against criteria?

For self-assessment, students need a clear concept of the learning goals and criteria (for example, what good writing looks like). They need skill at recognizing these characteristics in their own work when they see them: *To what extent does my writing exhibit these characteristics?* They need skill at translating their self-assessment judgments into action plans for improvement: *What does this evaluation suggest I should do next?*

Self-assessment skills, like any academic skills, should be taught. Ross, Hogaboam-Gray, and Rolheiser (2002) found that 5th and 6th graders who received 12 weeks of self-evaluation training in mathematics increased mathematics problem-solving achievement. Andrade, Du, & Wang (2008) found that 3rd and 4th grade students who self-assessed their writing increased the quality of their writing. These students did systematic self-assessment, using criteria and a rubric. A comparison group of students who just "looked over" their work did not improve as much.

Many teachers have students self-assess using rubrics or checklists. Teachers I have worked with often find some students take to self-assessment naturally, while others just check things without actually connecting their work with the criteria. Students who "get it" usually appreciate the opportunity to systematically go through their work (analysis), check it (evaluation), and fix it (creation). Students who don't, like the little boy in one 2nd grade class whose writing didn't satisfy the assignment but who checked "yes" on all the checklist questions anyway, can really benefit from some instruction and guided practice in self-assessment. They will learn the valuable skill of self-assessment, and they will also be learning and practicing higher-order thinking skills.

Self-assessment is for all subjects, not just mathematics and writing. Arem (2006) provides some sample assessments in physical education, specifically archery. She presents a series of four self- and peer assessments to increase students' understanding of good shooting form in archery and also to promote the kind of self-assessment and higher-order thinking that will help students become better learners. Students who have these opportunities to engage with their own learning, concentrate on progress, and give and receive feedback among peers, she notes, will become better archers. They will also develop higher-order thinking skills and become more independent learners.

Summing Up

This chapter presented ways to assess higher-order thinking according to a cognitive taxonomy. I used the top end of the Cognitive dimension of the revised Bloom's taxonomy to organize the chapter, but there are several other taxonomies I could have used. What they all have in common is that, as the number of elements (facts, concepts, statements, pieces of information) increases, and the number of relevant relationships among them increases, cognitive complexity increases. Students need to transfer their learning to contexts further and further from the one in which concepts were taught. Many curriculum documents and instructional materials use a cognitive taxonomy to ensure that higher-order thinking is taught and assessed, that students can transfer their knowledge to new situations.

The next chapters consider ways to assess students' logic and reasoning, judgment, problem solving, and creativity. Of course, these thinking skills are also important in a cognitive taxonomy. For example, in analyzing an author's argument and evaluating how successfully the author used various points to support it, a student makes deductions and critical appraisals. Nevertheless, considering logic, judgment, problem solving, and creativity separately helps, I think, to highlight the richness of the idea of "higher-order thinking." I hope the following chapters help you to build a broader repertoire of ways to assess higher-order thinking.

3 | Assessing Logic and Reasoning

Young children learn reasoning as part of life. For example, a father asks his 7-year-old son to make his bed in the morning before he leaves for school. The boy asks, "Why?" The father responds, "Because I said so." The boy may make the bed, but he will also be thinking, "That's not a reason." Or, for example, a mother drives past one gas station to fill up at another. Her daughter asks why, already reasoning that the closer station is more convenient. Her mother gives her another reason, "Because the gas is cheaper here," and the girl learns that reasons can be prioritized.

Reasoning skills can be honed and developed in school, even for young children. A kindergarten teacher I work with wrote in her journal that she emphasizes "how" and "why" questions with her students. She models thinking out loud, saying things like, "I wonder why they . . ." or "I wonder how that could be—it doesn't seem right." She writes: "I like it when they [her kindergarten students] are explaining something to me and they stop dead and say, 'Hey, that isn't right.'"

What Is Sound Reasoning?

Sound reasoning is required for the analytical, evaluative, and creative tasks we considered in Chapter 2 and, indeed, for all higher-order thinking. General reasoning skills include judging whether a single fact or claim is true and whether it is relevant to the argument or problem at hand, and judging whether two or more things are consistent. These skills are required for all types of reasoning. In this chapter, we discuss general reasoning skills and two basic kinds of specific reasoning: deduction and induction. All of these are important for thinking in school.

Deduction

Deduction means reasoning from a principle to an instance of the principle. In mathematics, for example, pre-algebra students learn that the commutative principle for addition states $a + b = b + a$. Therefore, by deduction, it must be true that $6 + 2 = 2 + 6$. Or in science, for example, elementary school students learn that plants need water in order to thrive. Therefore it follows, by deduction, that if the students don't water their sprouted lima bean seeds, the plants will die. One of the interesting features of deduction is that it is certain. If a principle is true, and if the deductive logic is applied correctly, the specific deduction must also be true. For example, given the commutative principle, 6 + 2 *must* equal 2 + 6.

In deduction, you start with one or more premises (the bases for the argument) and then use reasoning to come up with a conclusion. If the premises are not true, the conclusions may not be valid. If there are shaky assumptions behind the premises, the conclusions may not be valid. And if the conclusion does not follow from the premises, the conclusion may not be valid.

Identifying assumptions and premises. Sometimes premises are stated, and sometimes they are unstated assumptions. Consider this scenario about a 6th grade student. After lunch, recess was held indoors because it was raining. Students were in the gym shooting baskets or sitting and talking. The teacher on duty caught a girl taking the basketball from another student. The girl got in trouble. The teacher's reasoning went like this:

This girl took the boy's basketball.

People who take others' things should be punished.

Therefore, this girl should be punished.

The girl, however, protested. She said the teacher assumed the basketball belonged to the boy. In fact, she said, the boy had taken her ball before the teacher looked in their direction. The girl was just taking back the ball that was hers. Simple scenarios like this can help even young children learn what an *assumption* is and how to test for truth, relevance, and consistency in arguments.

Reasoning to a conclusion. Once the truth of premises and assumptions is established, students must use sound reasoning to arrive at conclusions. One thinking skill needed for sound deductive reasoning is the ability to decide what elements are logically a member of a class or category. Another is an understanding of what *conditions* mean, and the ability to reason using conditional logic (for example, using "if-then" logic, or distinguishing necessary from sufficient conditions). Yet another is understanding the meanings of *negative* and *partial*, and an ability to reason logically with these concepts (*and*, *or*, *not*, *double negatives*, *some*, and so on).

Simple "if-then" logic helps with deduction. Figure 3.1 (p. 64) presents and illustrates the four basic "if-then" forms, two of which are sound reasoning and two of which are not. Students can have fun playing with these ideas and develop their reasoning skills at the same time.

Induction

Induction involves reasoning from an instance or instances to a principle. Consider a classic analytical task like identifying the theme in an author's work and supporting the theme with evidence from the text. This is an inductive task, reasoning from various aspects of the text to what it might mean as a whole. Or consider hypothesis testing in science. Students write hypotheses based on theory, and an experiment is designed to test the hypothesis. Results are analyzed and interpreted according to whether they support or refute the hypothesis.

Figure 3.1 ✳ **"If-Then" Logic and Examples**

	Sound Reasoning	Unsound Reasoning
Positive	If A, then B. A is true. Therefore, B is true. If it is raining, Vanessa always carries an umbrella. It is raining. Therefore, Vanessa carries an umbrella.	If A, then B. B is true. Therefore, A is true. If it is raining, Vanessa always carries an umbrella. Vanessa is carrying an umbrella. Therefore, it is raining. **NOT NECESSARILY!** She could be carrying home a new umbrella she just bought at the store. Can you think of other reasons she might be carrying an umbrella when it's not raining?
Negative	If A, then B. B is not true. Therefore, A is not true. If it is raining, Vanessa always carries an umbrella. Vanessa is not carrying an umbrella today. Therefore, it must not be raining.	If A, then B. A is not true. Therefore, B is not true. If it is raining, Vanessa always carries an umbrella. It is not raining. Therefore, Vanessa is not carrying an umbrella. **NOT NECESSARILY!** It might be forecast to rain before she gets home from school. Can you think of other reasons she might carry an umbrella when it's not raining?

Reasoning from data, examples, and other information. Induction is reasoning from data, instances, specific examples, and other bits of information to generalize or extract a principle. Unlike deduction, inductive reasoning is not certain. For example, if students did a lot of commutative addition (showing that $6 + 2 = 2 + 6$, $5 + 3 = 3 + 5$, $17 + 46 = 46 + 17$, and so on), after a while most would be able to conclude, by induction, that $a + b = b + a$. But by induction alone, they could never be sure, because there would always be more addition sentences to try. As uncertain as this may sound, we actually learn quite a lot through induction. As I mentioned, the scientific method is based on inductive reasoning.

One thinking skill needed for sound inductive reasoning is the ability to see patterns in data or other evidence. Another is the ability to decide which conclusions best explain the patterns. In general, inductive thinking is about making appropriate inferences from evidence.

Reasoning by analogy. Another type of inductive reasoning is reasoning by analogy. This is reasoning based on the similarity of two things, and the quality of the reasoning depends on whether the two things are similar in ways that are really relevant to the argument. If you are tempted to say that only older children can do this, consider this childish argument: "But Dannette's mom lets her play outside after dinner!" The implied reasoning goes like this:

> I want permission to do something.
> Dannette's mom lets her do it.
> Dannette is a kid like me.
> I should have the same permission Dannette has.

This argument stands or falls on how much alike Dannette and her mother are to the protesting child and her parent. Is this little girl as responsible as Dannette? Is her mom's judgment based on the same principles of parenting that this little girl's family uses?

My point here isn't whether the little girl should be allowed to play outside after dinner or not; it's that she "naturally" uses reasoning by analogy. More academic reasoning by analogy can be taught by starting with students' basic understandings. Most students would easily be able to tell you, for example, that if the little girl was 5 years old and Dannette was 9, the little girl's appeal to her parents wouldn't be very compelling.

General Reasoning Skills

Deduction rests on premises, and induction rests on specific instances, but in both kinds of reasoning it is important to be able to discern that the principles or facts in question are each true and are each relevant to the problem or task. It is also important for students to be able to identify consistencies and inconsistencies among the ideas they put together. Sloppy thinking results in poor understanding and poor work. If you are a classroom teacher, you have undoubtedly read some student work where the "supporting evidence from the text," for example, does not, in fact, support the conclusion the student claims it does.

Reasoning skills are important and should be taught from a young age—they should not be saved until students are ready for the finer points in a discipline. I know a 1st grade learning support teacher whose students had read a story called "The Seed." The teacher had asked them to finish the sentence "I like this book because . . . ." One student wrote, "I like to plant seeds." Another student wrote, "It is fune [sic]."

Student 1's reason was more closely relevant, and students even at this developmental level can begin to consider which reason more strongly supports a statement about liking the book. Enjoying the topic of the book is a specific and relevant reason for liking the book. "It is fun," on the other hand, basically just restates "I like the book." An older student would call this a circular argument.

Logical Errors

Common errors in logic are often presented to freshman composition classes in college as an aid to strengthening students' writing. The reasoning behind many of these "logical fallacies" are simple enough that younger students can understand them. Figure 3.2 presents several of the classic fallacies in simple language and includes examples that can be used with younger students.

Note that these are only a selection of the common logical fallacies. I have selected these because the reasoning involved is accessible to young students. As students begin to understand how to analyze reasoning, they will be able to handle more complex examples. The point here is that even young students can learn to ask whether reasoning is based on things that are true, relevant, and consistent.

Figure 3.2 ✳ **Some Common Errors in Logic**

Logical Error and Definition	Example of Poor Reasoning	Example of Good Reasoning
Overgeneralizing Reasoning from one or a very few examples to a whole group.	Billy and DeShaun are bullies. They push other kids around and take things from them. It must be because they're boys. I'm going to stay away from all the boys on the playground.	Billy and DeShaun are bullies. They push other kids around and take things from them. I'm going to stay away from Billy and DeShaun on the playground.
Appeal to Authority Reasoning that because an important figure believes or does something, it is true, good, or important.	A famous movie star says I should smoke this brand of cigarettes. He's cool, so smoking these cigarettes must be cool, too.	My doctor says I shouldn't smoke cigarettes. He has read studies that show smoking causes cancer, and he doesn't want me to get cancer.
Social Acceptability (In Latin, *ad populum* argument, sometimes called the "bandwagon argument") Reasoning that something is true because lots of people believe it or that something is good because lots of people do it.	All my friends tell me *American Idol* is the best TV show to watch. I should watch it. I'll love it.	I really like watching *American Idol* because I like music and comedy. I also like trying to guess who the audience will like and what the judges will say.
Against the Person (In Latin, *ad hominem* argument)	Lisa says that the animal shelter is a great place to volunteer. But Lisa is such a freak. She wears such funny clothes and is such a loner. She's probably wrong, and I wouldn't like it.	Lisa says that the animal shelter is a great place to volunteer. I like animals, so I might try volunteering and see if I like it.
Straw Man Reasoning by setting up a simple-minded or watered-down version of your opponent's argument, knocking it down easily, and then claiming your side of the argument is therefore right.	My parents give me an allowance, but they only want me to spend it on things I need and save the rest. That's dumb—then why give me an allowance? I should be able to spend it on anything I want.	My parents give me an allowance, but they want me to think carefully about the things I spend money on, and save some, too. But I think I should be able to spend my allowance on anything I want, because once they give it to me, it's my money.

Assessing Logic and Reasoning

As with other higher-order-thinking assessments, to assess reasoning you first have to give students something to reason *about*. Supply introductory material for multiple-choice, short-answer, and essay questions. For longer performance assessments and projects, you could also allow students access to resources they have already seen (for example, a book or textbook they have read) or ask them to locate resources (for example, finding information in a library or on the Internet). Then ask questions that require students to reason about the material.

Make or Evaluate a Deductive Conclusion

To assess how students make or evaluate deductive conclusions, give them a statement they are to assume is true and one or more logically correct and incorrect conclusions. Then ask them which conclusions follow. The following example shows several different methods of assessing students' abilities to make deductive conclusions from the statements in the Bill of Rights. All these assessment examples require reasoning from the principles (such as freedom of religion, freedom of speech, and so on) to specific instances of them. These assessment examples differ in format and in amount of writing required.

Bill of Rights of the United States Constitution

AMENDMENT 1.
Congress shall make no law respecting an establishment of religion, or prohibiting the free exercise thereof; or abridging the freedom of speech, or of the press; or the right of the people peaceably to assemble, and to petition the Government for a redress of grievances.

AMENDMENT 2.
A well regulated Militia, being necessary to the security of a free State, the right of the people to keep and bear Arms, shall not be infringed.

AMENDMENT 3.
No Soldier shall in time of peace be quartered in any house, without the consent of the Owner, nor in time of war, but in a manner to be prescribed by law.

AMENDMENT 4.

The right of the people to be secure in their persons, houses, papers, and effects, against unreasonable searches and seizures, shall not be violated, and no warrants shall issue, but upon probable cause, supported by Oath or affirmation, and particularly describing the place to be searched, and the persons or things to be seized.

AMENDMENT 5.

No person shall be held to answer for a capital, or otherwise infamous crime, unless on a presentment or indictment of a Grand Jury, except in cases arising in the land or naval forces, or in the Militia, when in actual service in time of War or public danger; nor shall any person be subject for the same offense to be twice put in jeopardy of life or limb; nor shall be compelled in any criminal case to be a witness against himself, nor be deprived of life, liberty, or property, without due process of law; nor shall private property be taken for public use, without just compensation.

AMENDMENT 6.

In all criminal prosecutions, the accused shall enjoy the right to a speedy and public trial, by an impartial jury of the State and district wherein the crime shall have been committed, which district shall have been previously ascertained by law, and to be informed of the nature and cause of the accusation; to be confronted with the witnesses against him; to have compulsory process for obtaining witnesses in his favor, and to have the assistance of counsel for his defense.

AMENDMENT 7.

In Suits at common law, where the value in controversy shall exceed twenty dollars, the right of trial by jury shall be preserved, and no fact tried by a jury, shall be otherwise re-examined in any Court of the United States, than according to the rules of the common law.

AMENDMENT 8.

Excessive bail shall not be required, nor excessive fines imposed, nor cruel and unusual punishments inflicted.

AMENDMENT 9.

The enumeration in the Constitution, of certain rights, shall not be construed to deny or disparage others retained by the people.

AMENDMENT 10.

The powers not delegated to the United States by the Constitution, nor prohibited by it to the States, are reserved to the States respectively, or to the people.

continued

Multiple-choice questions assessing the ability to make deductive conclusions

1. Which of the following scenarios describes behavior that is legal because of the First Amendment?

    A. Mr. Jones threw a rock through the front window of Mr. Smith's house. Around the rock was tied a paper that called Mr. Smith nasty names.

    B. Mr. Jones waited until Mr. Smith left for work one morning, then got in his car and followed him, honking and yelling.

    C. Mr. Jones doesn't trust his neighbor, Mr. Smith. Jones believes Smith is a dangerous person and a threat to the peace of the neighborhood. Therefore, Mr. Jones buys a gun.

    *D. Mr. Jones wrote a letter to the editor of the local paper. Mr. Smith heads a local environmental committee, and Mr. Jones called his position "disastrous."

2. Ms. Gutierrez owns a small house near an interstate highway. She and her family have lived there for three years. The state highway department wanted to put in a new intersection, so they condemned all the property required for construction of the intersection and told the owners that they would pay them each half of what their property was worth. Ms. Gutierrez could challenge the state by citing which amendment?

    A. Fourth Amendment
    *B. Fifth Amendment
    C. Sixth Amendment
    D. Seventh Amendment

Essay questions assessing the ability to make deductive conclusions

3. Select one of the amendments in the Bill of Rights of the U.S. Constitution. Describe a specific example of one of the rights in the Bill of Rights. The example can be from a real event or something you make

up yourself, but it must be a clear illustration of one of the rights in the Bill of Rights. Tell the story of your example. Then explain which right your story exemplifies, from which amendment, and tell why.

CRITERIA for feedback or rubrics:

- Appropriate identification of a particular right and amendment.
- Appropriateness of example.
- Appropriateness of evidence.
- Soundness of reasoning and clarity of explanation.

4. Mr. Jones wrote a letter to the editor of the local paper. Mr. Smith heads a local environmental committee, and Mr. Jones called his position "disastrous" for the local economy. The letter attacked not only the committee's position but Mr. Smith personally, calling him "ridiculous" and "stupid." Neither Mr. Smith nor the committee responded, so Mr. Jones threw a rock through the front window of Mr. Smith's house. Around the rock he had tied the editorial page from the paper, with his letter to the editor printed on it.

    According to the Bill of Rights of the U.S. Constitution, was Mr. Jones within his rights for any of the actions he took? Did he exceed the boundaries of protected behavior at any point? Explain your reasoning. In your explanation, refer to specific amendment(s) and right(s) and tell how they relate to Mr. Jones's story.

CRITERIA for feedback or rubrics:

- Identification of First Amendment, free speech.
- Appropriateness of evidence.
- Soundness of reasoning and clarity of explanation.

Performance assessment assessing the ability to make deductive conclusions

5. Make a notebook with a section for each amendment in the Bill of Rights. Using news stories from newspapers, news magazines,

continued

and the Internet, illustrate each amendment with at least one specific example of the exercise of this right. Include a copy of each news story, cut from the paper or printed from the Internet. For each story, write a brief essay explaining what specific amendment(s) and right(s) are illustrated, and explain your reasoning.

CRITERIA for feedback or rubrics:

- Appropriateness and completeness of illustrations/examples/ news stories.
- Appropriateness of evidence.
- Soundness of reasoning and clarity of explanation.

Multiple-choice questions would be scored right or wrong and used in class formatively or on a test for a grade. If the essay questions are used formatively, the criteria can be used to frame feedback and guide student self- or peer assessment. If the essay questions are to be scored as part of a test, for a grade, the criteria can be made into holistic or analytic rubrics, as in the Declaration of Independence examples in Chapter 2. The criteria for the performance assessment also can be made into holistic or analytic rubrics. Because the performance assessment asks students to make a notebook with 10 sections, one for each amendment, each section could be scored separately. Scoring by section would give students more specific information about the details of the work they did. Alternatively, rubrics could be applied to the performance assessment (the notebook) as a whole.

The assessment examples in each format (multiple-choice, essay, and performance assessment) call for deduction in the form of reasoning from the principles in the Bill of Rights to specific examples of what they mean for real-life situations. However, these three formats are not interchangeable. The multiple-choice questions require reading and reasoning. The essay questions require reading, reasoning, and writing. The performance assessment requires reading, reasoning, locating resource material, writing, and extended planning.

A very common way of evaluating deductive reasoning in mathematics is asking students to do algebraic proofs. Here is an example:

Show that $[(x + 2) 3] + 6 = 3 (x + 4)$
To show that this equality is true, the student would have to list a series of specific reasoning steps, each justified by application of an algebraic principle.

$[(x + 2) 3] + 6 =$	
$[(x \bullet 3) + (2 \bullet 3)] + 6 =$	Distributive principle for multiplication over addition
$[3x + (2 \bullet 3)] + 6 =$	Commutative principle for multiplication
$(3x + 6) + 6 =$	Computation, $2 \bullet 3 = 6$
$3x + (6 + 6) =$	Associative principle for addition
$3x + 12 =$	Computation, $6 + 6 = 12$
$3x + (3 \bullet 4) =$	Substitution, $12 = 3 \bullet 4$
$3 (x + 4)$	Left distributive principle for multiplication over addition

If the student appropriately applied each principle, the equality is true for all values of x. And more important, the student has demonstrated the ability to think deductively in mathematics. Notice that once again, content knowledge and reasoning are required to answer this question. The student needs to know the distributive, associative, and commutative principles and basic computational facts.

Because deductive reasoning is certain, it takes only one counter-example to disprove a deduction. The following is an example of a multiple-choice question that assesses this understanding, as well as content understanding about rectangles and other geometric shapes:

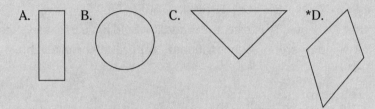

7. Alan says that if a figure has four sides, it must be a rectangle. Gina does not agree. Which of the following figures shows that Gina is correct?

A.   B.   C.   *D.

Source: National Assessment of Educational Progress, Mathematics, grade 4, Block 2003-4M6, no. 7. Available: http://nces.ed.gov/nationsreportcard/itmrlsx/landing.aspx

In addition to understanding the logic of counter-examples to select the correct answer, students can use other types of logical reasoning to eliminate the incorrect ones. Choice A supports Alan's claim, and the question requires refuting it. Choices B and C are not relevant to the argument because these figures do not have four sides. Students who reason in this way are using several thinking skills. First, using the logic of class inclusion mentioned above, they decide what elements are logically a member of a class or category, and then they reason from the requirements of Alan's and Gina's argument that if the figures are not members of the "four-sided" category, they are not relevant.

Make or Evaluate an Inductive Conclusion

To assess how students make or evaluate inductive conclusions, give them a scenario and some information. Then ask them to draw the proper conclusion from the information and explain why the conclusion is correct. For multiple-choice items, have students select from among alternative conclusions.

Examples of reasoning by induction. The 9th grade science assessment of thinking about chemical and physical changes in Chapter 1 is an example of assessing inductive thinking. Students drew conclusions about chemical and physical changes by looking at the characteristics of examples of each. The students whose reasoning was deepest and most complete—the ones who figured out that if you could "get it [a substance] back the way it was" then the change was physical, otherwise it was chemical—were also the ones whom the teacher assessed as most completely understanding the concept. Reasoning and learning go hand in hand.

The "interpretation of results" sections of science lab reports are usually assessments of inductive reasoning. Students are asked to interpret what their results mean in light of their research questions and hypotheses. Lab reports are a kind of performance assessment. Make sure the criteria you use for feedback and scoring include a consideration of the soundness of students' reasoning as they interpret their results.

In the social sciences, too, students demonstrate inductive thinking when they interpret results. Here is an example of interpreting results in social studies. More examples of reasoning from data appear in Chapter 5, which is about problem solving.

Question 4 refers to the bar graph below.

Reported Voter Turnout by Average Income, 1992
(as a percentage of voting-age population)

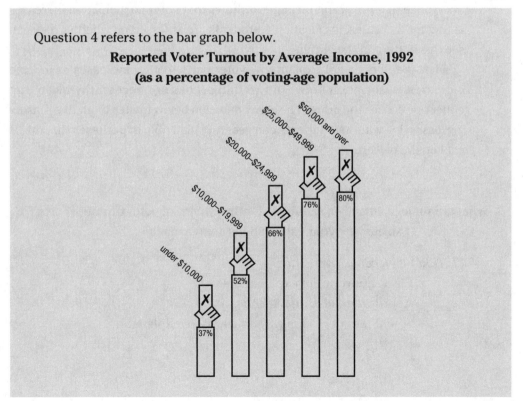

continued

4. The graph shows that

    A. wealthy people tend to have different political views than do people with less money.

    B. the incomes of certain groups of voters have increased dramatically.

   *C. the higher someone's income is, the more likely he or she is to vote.

    D. young people are more likely to vote than are older people.

Source: National Assessment of Educational Progress, Civics, grade 8, Block 1998-8C3, nos. 4–5. Available: http://nces.ed.gov/nationsreportcard/itmrlsx/landing.aspx

Notice that the graph on page 75 shows that voter participation increases as income increases. In Question 4, students are assessed on whether they can see this pattern in the graph.

The graph does not explain *why* voter participation increases as income increases. Association between two things does not necessarily mean that either one causes the other. The essay question below invites inductive reasoning, assessing whether students can generate plausible hypotheses that might explain the pattern.

What are some plausible explanations for the pattern of voter turnout shown in the graph? Explain why your explanations are reasonable.

CRITERIA for feedback or rubrics:
- Clear, appropriate explanation(s).
- Appropriateness of evidence.
- Soundness of reasoning and clarity of explanation.

Here are examples of hypotheses that follow logically:

• Higher-income people might have more education and be more likely to recognize the importance of voting.

• Higher-income people may be more confident in the political system or feel they have more at stake in the system under which they have been successful.

• Lower-income people may think that politicians don't really care about them or think their votes don't matter.

• Younger people tend to have lower incomes than older people, and voter participation rates for younger people are less than for older people.

Hypotheses that represent faulty reasoning would include statements that do not follow logically—for example, saying lower-income people don't have enough time (higher-income people could be just as busy); statements that are circular arguments—for example, saying higher-income people vote more (which just restates what the graph shows); and statements that are irrelevant—for example, saying that lower-income people don't go on fancy vacations.

For a longer and more in-depth essay, you might add an additional question:

What additional evidence might you collect to figure out which of these explanations is more likely to be the cause of the relationship between income and voter turnout in 1992?

CRITERIA for feedback or rubrics:

• Clear, appropriate suggestions for additional evidence to collect.
• Soundness of reasoning about how the hypotheses would be tested.
• Clarity of explanation.

You would assess students' responses according to whether the additional evidence they suggest (for example, interviews of a sample of high- and low-income people who voted and didn't vote in 1992) is relevant to investigating the hypotheses they suggested, and how well they explained why. Use the criteria as the basis for feedback and for creating holistic or analytic rubrics.

Example of reasoning by analogy. History teachers implicitly invite reasoning by analogy when they make pronouncements such as this: "Those who do not learn history are condemned to repeat it." Project assignments or test questions that ask students to see historical parallels require inductive thinking. Questions that present two historical events and ask students to point out the parallels would be Analyze-level questions in Bloom's taxonomy. Questions that ask students to project the parallels themselves would be at the Evaluate or Create level. Here is an example:

After World War II, George C. Marshall (U.S. secretary of state, 1947–1949) won a Nobel Peace Prize for his work on the Marshall Plan, which supported postwar economic recovery for 16 countries. First, describe how the Marshall Plan worked. Then, select one of these more recent conflicts in which the U.S. was involved:

- Korean War (1950–1953)
- Vietnam War (1959–1975)
- Persian Gulf War (1990–1991)

How were postwar conditions for the conflict you selected similar to or different from post–World War II conditions? What might have happened if the United States had instituted a "Marshall-like" plan at that time? Explain your reasoning.

CRITERIA for feedback or rubrics for description of the Marshall Plan:

- Complete and accurate summary of the function of the Marshall Plan.
- Clarity of explanation.

CRITERIA for feedback or rubrics for the "what if" question:

- Clear, appropriate thesis about what might have happened.
- Accurate recounting of relevant historical details.
- Appropriateness of evidence regarding similarities and differences between post-WWII and postwar conditions for the conflict selected.
- Soundness of reasoning and clarity of explanation.

This task assesses recall of information about the Marshall Plan and analysis of similarities and differences between World War II and another war. The "what if" question requires students to create their own scenarios. Their explanations might also demonstrate some evaluation of the plausibility of their scenarios. You would assess students' reasoning according to both how logical their reasoning was and how relevant the evidence was. As before, criteria could be used to support feedback and to develop holistic or analytic rubrics for formative or summative use.

In most classrooms, this assignment would probably work better as a performance assessment, giving students time to go to the library to use the Internet and other sources to look up information. Students could do a more thorough and thoughtful analysis of the similarities and differences between postwar conditions, and reason about the potential results of supporting postwar economic recovery, if they had access to more information than they would be able to hold in memory. In fact, this could turn into a major project requiring library and Internet research, higher-order thinking, and writing.

For major projects, rubrics should specifically include reference to student thinking, just as they should for essay questions and smaller-scale performance assessments. Figure 3.3 (pp. 80–81) presents a set of general rubrics for written projects. Notice that the content rubric talks about the accuracy of facts and details and the completeness of information, both in the context of whether the thesis is clear and logically supported. Thinking cannot be done in the abstract. Students must think about something. The accuracy and relevance of what they

Figure 3.3 ✳ **General Rubrics for Written Projects**

	CONTENT	REASONING & EVIDENCE	CLARITY OF WRITTEN EXPRESSION
4	The thesis is clear. A large amount and variety of material and evidence support the thesis. All material is relevant. This material includes details. Information is accurate. Appropriate sources were consulted.	Information is clearly and explicitly related to the point(s) the material is intended to support. Information is organized in a logical manner and is presented concisely. Flow is good. Introductions, transitions, and other connecting material take the listener/reader along.	Few errors of grammar and usage; any minor errors do not interfere with meaning. Language style and word choice are highly effective and enhance meaning. Style and word choice are appropriate to the project.
3	The thesis is clear. An adequate amount of material and evidence supports the thesis. Most material is relevant. This material includes details. Information is mostly accurate; any inaccuracies are minor and do not interfere with the points made. Appropriate sources were consulted.	Information is clearly related to the point(s) the material is intended to support, although not all connections may be explained. Information is organized in a logical manner. Flow is adequate. Introductions, transitions, and other connecting material take the listener/reader along for the most part. Any abrupt transitions do not interfere with intended meaning.	Some errors of grammar and usage; errors do not interfere with meaning. Language style and word choice are for the most part effective and appropriate to the project.
2	The thesis may be somewhat unclear. Some material and evidence support the thesis. Some of the material is relevant, and some is not. Details are lacking. Information may include some inaccuracies. At least some sources were appropriate.	Some of the information is related to the point(s) the material is intended to support, but connections are not explained. Information is not entirely organized in a logical manner, although some structure is apparent. Flow is choppy. Introductions, transitions, and other connecting material may be lacking or unsuccessful.	Major errors of grammar and usage begin to interfere with meaning. Language style and word choice are simple, bland, or otherwise not very effective or not entirely appropriate.

	CONTENT	REASONING & EVIDENCE	CLARITY OF WRITTEN EXPRESSION
1	The thesis is not clear. Much of the material may be irrelevant to the overall topic or inaccurate. Details are lacking. Appropriate sources were not consulted.	Information is not related to the point(s) the material is intended to support. Information is not organized in a logical manner. Material does not flow. Information is presented as a sequence of unrelated material.	Major errors of grammar and usage make meaning unclear. Language style and word choice are ineffective and/or inappropriate.

Source: Adapted from *How to Give Effective Feedback to Your Students* (pp. 63–64), by S. M. Brookhart, 2008, Alexandria, VA: ASCD. © 2008 by ASCD.

think about is tied up with their reasoning. In fact, judging the accuracy and relevance of information is part of the reasoning process.

To use this assignment as a performance assessment, you would add directions about length, number and type of sources to be consulted, and due date. You would build in several opportunities for partial products to be formatively assessed (see the following section).

Formative and Summative Uses of Results

Chapter 2 discussed formative ways to use multiple-choice questions, with classroom-response systems or ABCD cards and follow-up discussions and activities in class. These continue to be good formative strategies for questions like the voter turnout item. To use questions like this to improve students' reasoning skills, it is important to make sure that in the follow-up discussions students talk about their reasoning. Why did they choose a particular option? As students discuss these choices, they will clarify the reasoning involved. In Chapter 2 we also discussed giving feedback on essays that includes comments about students' reasoning.

The Marshall Plan performance assessment is an example of a long-term project assessing higher-order thinking. Build formative assessment opportunities into student work on long-term projects by assessing plans, progress, or partial products. Don't make students wait until the end of a long assignment to get information about how the work is contributing to their learning. I certainly remember lots of term paper–type assignments in high school where the only assistance the teacher gave was to schedule "library days" so that we could locate information. But most of the time, the assignment was given and students were left alone to work on it until the due date, when we handed it in.

A more effective use of a long-term assignment, from an assessment perspective, is to build in formative opportunities while work on the final product is still ongoing. This approach is especially important for the thinking process. Students won't intentionally write unclear theses or poorly support their positions. And if the first time they know they have done so is at the end of the work period, it's too late to clarify the thinking or improve the product.

In your directions for the Marshall Plan performance assessment, you could build in partial products to be assessed formatively. You could require an outline of what the students are going to write as the answer to the first part of the question (describing the Marshall Plan). This outline could be the subject of self-assessment, peer assessment, teacher feedback, or any combination of those. You could require a one-paragraph statement of the thesis students choose, identifying which more recent conflict they have selected and their major conclusion about the similarities and differences relevant to economic recovery, and the major support they are going to give in their paper. You could require a planning document with or after this paragraph, describing students' strategies for locating the additional information they will need to finish their papers. Again, either of these requirements could be the subject of self- or peer assessment and teacher feedback.

The important formative point here is that the information students receive from reflecting on their partial products and from feedback on their partial products can be incorporated into their work going forward. Then, when the time for summative assessment comes, the characteristics in the rubric will be better understood—and better met—than if no on-the-way formative assessment had taken place.

Summing Up

Reasoning is required for all higher-order thinking, so in some senses this chapter overlaps all the others. This chapter has discussed logic and reasoning separately because reasoning itself—what it is, how to do it, and how to write assessment items and tasks that call for it—is not explicitly discussed as often as some of the other topics in this book. Much is made of cognitive taxonomies and problem solving, for example, but the mental infrastructure students need is less often discussed.

I hope that this chapter has given you some ideas for how to make the mechanics of thinking visible to students and how to write assessment items and tasks that will help you and your students figure out what kinds of reasoning they can do with what level of skill. As we turn in Chapter 4 to students' critical thinking and judgment, you should be all set to keep in mind the logic and reasoning needed to support that critical thinking.

4 | Assessing Judgment

One kind of higher-order thinking is "critical thinking" in the sense of applying prudent or wise judgment to a situation. The Norris and Ennis (1989) definition quoted earlier—"Critical thinking is reasonable, reflective thinking that is focused on deciding what to believe or do" (p. 3)—emphasizes this aspect of higher-order thinking. We all hope that our students turn out to have these qualities of good judgment, prudence, and wisdom.

Such qualities are important for good academic work, for instance in distinguishing among more and less credible historical accounts, or distinguishing among more and less appealing uses of a particular literary device by an author. Examples of the kind of judgment that students are asked to exercise in school include judging the credibility of a source (especially important in the Internet age); figuring out what an advertiser for a product, service, or candidate wants the reader or viewer to believe and what persuasive methods are used; appraising the usefulness of a text or a concept for one's own life and purposes; and deciding what to say or how to say something in various academic and classroom situations.

These qualities are also important in other aspects of life. Parents and teachers often express this reality when they talk about wanting their children or students to "make good choices."

What Is Good Judgment?

Good judgment can be a very practical skill. Do you remember being taught "If it sounds too good to be true, it probably is"? What if someone sends you an e-mail telling you that a foreign industrialist has just left you a million dollars, and all you have to do is send your bank account number, log-in, and password in order to transfer the funds? To exercise good judgment about how credible this is, you need to be able to ask yourself how likely it is that a foreign industrialist whom you don't know would have left you anything, let alone a million dollars. You need to understand the risks associated with divulging identifying information, and the motivation some people might have in asking for it. And then you need to conclude, "This e-mail is fraudulent, and I should delete it."

Good judgment can help keep you from being led down other primrose paths, as well. I remember from my own school days a high school social studies unit titled "Developing a Crap Detector." I won't tell you how long ago that was, but suffice it to say it was before the Internet age. Advertisements—memorably, the Marlboro Man—were the vehicle for this unit on critical thinking, and we were encouraged to ask what the advertisers meant to communicate and what their motives might be. The goal, of course, was to make my class of teenagers a little less gullible and susceptible to glossy ads suggesting that we would be cool, sexy, or popular if we only bought some product or other. I remember that unit in part because it was fun, but also because my class hadn't been explicitly taught to think like that before, and it surprised me. It had never occurred to me that this kind of wisdom was part of being "school smart." And that's really too bad. I recommend asking even very young students to think about what to believe or do, and explain why.

Judging the credibility of a source of information is an important aspect of good judgment. How much faith should you put in the results of Internet searches? How can you find out by what authority or from what background, training, and experience an author writes? How can you evaluate whether that authority or particular background actually does give an author the footing from which to speak on some issue? What is an author's vested interest or point of view? How did an author get his or her information? What's the difference between a newspaper and a tabloid? Between a journal and a magazine? Questions like these are important for the kind of research students do in libraries for term papers and projects. And although the Internet makes judging the credibility of information especially significant now, this has really always been an important skill.

In Chapter 2, we talked about the kind of judgment required for tasks at the Evaluate level of Bloom's taxonomy. When we ask students to evaluate how well the author of a speech succeeds in using imagery to make his or her point or how important it will be to pay attention to environmental issues in the next election, we also ask them to use reasoned judgment.

Assessing Judgment

To assess students' use of critical judgment, give them a scenario, a speech, an advertisement, or other source of information. Then ask them to make some sort of critical judgment. The kinds of judgments we consider here include evaluating the credibility of a source of information, identifying assumptions implicit in that information, and identifying rhetorical and persuasive methods.

Evaluate the Credibility of a Source

Evaluating the credibility of a source has received a lot more attention since the Internet age began. But even before the Internet, teachers often repeated to students, "Just because something is printed in black and white doesn't mean it's true." The explosion of information available electronically means students need to be able to judge the credibility of an ever-widening array of sources.

To assess how students judge the credibility of a source, give students material to think about. Then ask them which parts, if any, of the material are credible, which parts aren't, and why.

Patrick Mulroy, a business and computer teacher at Ford City High School in Pennsylvania, taught and then assessed his 9th grade class on evaluating the credibility of electronic resources. Groups of students looked at three Web sites. They decided whether they believed these Web sites would be good sources of information for school projects. As part of instruction, Patrick gave students the following questions to help them think:

- If you wanted to obtain more information about this Web site, whom could you contact?
- What other resources could you use to back up or corroborate information presented on this Web site?
- How can you tell if the information contained on this Web site is true or false?

The assessment came when each group created a list of five questions they could use to evaluate any Web site, applied them to one of the Web sites they had discussed, and wrote a paragraph explaining why they would or would not choose that Web site for use in a school project.

The teacher modeled asking evaluative questions about Web sites as he circulated among the groups doing their work. He adjusted the level of modeling and assistance, increasing it for more novice classes and decreasing it for classes of students with more experience judging the credibility of Web sites. Successful groups came up with questions like the following: When was the Web site last updated? Who is the author of the Web content? What are that person's qualifications or credentials? Who sponsors the Web site? What is the copyright date? How do the pictures relate to the topic?

Based on their answers to these kinds of questions, students decided whether or not to recommend the Web site they wrote about. In each group's work, Patrick looked for sound criteria, appropriate application of the criteria to the particular Web site, and a reasonable conclusion about how to use the Web site (or not) in school projects.

Although this example comes from a computer class, students from any subject matter class in which research projects are done could evaluate the credibility of Web sites they would use for information for their reports. That spectrum basically means any discipline, from humanities to the arts, science and math, physical education and consumer science, business and trades. The teacher could provide a list of Web sites to work with, or students could generate their own list using search engines.

Identify Implicit Assumptions

Identifying what is assumed in an argument or text is an important skill in itself. Examining assumptions also helps students judge the soundness of arguments, as we discussed in Chapter 3. Assessment of students' ability to identify assumptions in most subject area content often can be accomplished with either multiple-choice questions or brief constructed-response (short-answer) questions.

To use a multiple-choice item to assess how students identify implicit assumptions, give them an argument or explanation that has some unstated assumptions. Offer one choice that is a correct implicit assumption and two or more choices that are neither the implicit assumption nor conclusions. Ask students which option is probably assumed or taken for granted. To use a constructed-response item, give students the material and ask them directly to identify implicit assumptions and explain their reasoning. In the following example, either could be done. Note, however, that the multiple-choice version assesses whether students can recognize the assumption, and the constructed-response version assesses whether students can generate the assumption themselves.

Multiple-choice version

A marketing executive for a sports shoe company wanted to make the most of his advertising budget. He decided to buy advertising time on television sports broadcasts, reasoning that many people who watched sports would also like to play sports, and therefore need sports shoes. What assumption has to be true in order for this argument to represent sound thinking?

A. More men than women watch TV sports, and more men than women buy sports shoes.

B. People will want to buy the shoes they see professional athletes wearing during their games.

*C. People who don't watch sports don't buy sports shoes as frequently as those who do.

Multiple-choice version with explanation

Give students the previous multiple-choice question, then ask them to write a sentence or two explaining the reasoning behind their choice.

Short-answer version

Give students the question (without the choices), with this additional sentence: Explain your reasoning.

CRITERIA for feedback or rubrics:

- Clear, appropriate statement of underlying assumption.
- Appropriateness of evidence.
- Soundness of reasoning and clarity of explanation.

As before, use the criteria as a framework for feedback and for constructing holistic or analytic rubrics.

Identifying assumptions is a useful skill in many disciplines. In social studies, students can identify assumptions behind newspaper articles covering local or national events, political speeches and commentary, and the like. For example, you might select a local editorial about an upcoming school levy, and ask students to read it and identify assumptions. The assumptions might be things like "education is important for economic growth in the community," or "it is more important to keep money in the hands of individuals than to use it for community purposes," and so on.

In addition to identifying assumptions underlying issues in current events, students can identify assumptions in historical contexts. Here is an example from the U.S. Civil War era:

Lincoln delivered his Gettysburg Address in 1863, at the dedication of Soldiers' National Cemetery in Gettysburg, Pennsylvania. Here are the first two paragraphs:

> Four score and seven years ago our fathers brought forth on this continent a new nation, conceived in Liberty, and dedicated to the proposition that all men are created equal.
>
> Now we are engaged in a great civil war, testing whether that nation, or any nation so conceived and so dedicated, can long endure. We are met on a great battlefield of that war. We have come to dedicate a portion of that field, as a final resting place for those who here gave their lives that that nation might live. It is altogether fitting and proper that we should do this.

What assumptions about the Civil War are implicit in this section of the speech? Identify these, and explain how the text supports these assumptions. How do these assumptions compare with current-day historians' views of the Civil War?

CRITERIA for feedback or rubrics:

- Clear, appropriate statement of underlying assumptions in Lincoln's speech.
- Clear thesis statement about how these assumptions compare with current-day views.
- Appropriateness of evidence.
- Soundness of reasoning and clarity of explanation.

The first part of the question, about Lincoln's characterization of the Civil War in his speech, asks students to identify implicit assumptions. Assess students on how well they identify the assumptions and how well they explain the basis of their inferences in the text. The second part of the question, asking how Lincoln's view of the war inferred from the speech compares with current-day scholars' views of the war, is an analysis task (see Chapter 3). Assess students on their understanding of current views on the Civil War and on the soundness of their comparison with Lincoln's perspective. As you now—I hope!—know, use the criteria to focus your feedback and to create holistic or analytic rubrics for this assessment.

In English/language arts, students can identify assumptions that characters in novels or short stories make about the world or their situation, motivating their actions. For example, many Jane Austen novels include social commentary about the conventions of the times. Students in the 21st century live under very different social conditions and conventions from those common in the early 19th century. If students are reading *Pride and Prejudice* in their English class, you could ask them to identify assumptions about how men and women in various classes of society were expected to act, and how they could tell from the novel. Assess them on the soundness of their inferences from events, actions, and dialogue to the underlying social expectations.

For short-essay questions about identifying assumptions, you can adapt the analytic rubrics in Chapter 2 presented as part of the Declaration of Independence example that involves "identifying the main point." Instead of assessing whether the thesis reflects the main point of the argument, assess whether the thesis accurately identifies implicit assumption(s) in the text. Figure 4.1 (p. 92) suggests a way to do that, and also shows how this rubric can be adapted to various other higher-order thinking tasks that result in a thesis, a statement of students' conclusions that they will go on to support with evidence and reasoning.

Identify Rhetorical and Persuasive Strategies

You may think of identifying rhetorical tactics as an aspect of literary analysis. This kind of judgment is actually important for communications of all sorts, from news media, advertisers, political campaigns, and historical accounts.

Figure 4.1 ✳ **General Rubric for Critical Thinking Involving Judgment**

	2	1	0
Thesis (judgment of credibility, identification of assumption or persuasive tactic, etc.)	Thesis is clear, is complete, and answers the question posed by the problem or task.	Thesis is clear and at least partially answers the question posed by the problem or task.	Thesis is not clear or does not answer the question posed by the problem or task.
Evidence	Evidence is accurate, relevant, and complete.	Evidence is mostly clear, relevant, and complete.	Evidence is not clear, relevant, or complete.
Reasoning and clarity	The way in which the evidence supports the thesis is clear, logical, and well explained.	The way in which the evidence supports the thesis is mostly clear and logical. Some explanation is given.	The way in which the evidence supports the thesis is not clear, is illogical, or is not explained.

To assess how students identify persuasive communications, give students the text of a speech, an advertisement in any medium, an editorial, or any other persuasive communication. Then ask students what statements or strategies the author uses, what effects the author expects these strategies to have, and whether any of the statements or strategies are deceptive or misleading. In multiple-choice exercises, students select answers, and in constructed-response exercises, students can explain their reasoning. Here is a famous example of the use of persuasive tactics.

12. The poster shown above was made during the First World War. What was the poster designed to do?

    A. Make people feel that it would be easy to win the war.

    B. Make people feel guilty for thinking that war is harmful.

    C. Get people to join the army by making them feel responsible for starting the war.

    *D. Get people to join the army by appealing to patriotic feelings.

Test-item source: National Assessment of Educational Progress, Civics, grade 8, Block 1998-8C10, no. 12. Available: http://nces.ed.gov/nationsreportcard/itmrlsx/landing.aspx

Poster source: Library of Congress. Public domain.

To answer this question, students would have to identify Uncle Sam and recognize the strategy used in the poster. Uncle Sam points his finger at the viewer, in an authoritative gesture of selection. When mom or dad does something similar ("I want YOU to take out the garbage"), it's an authoritative appeal to duty, as well, but not as appealing. When Uncle Sam does it, it's an authoritative appeal to duty, but one to which patriotic viewers might feel honored to respond.

The multiple-choice version of this question assesses students' abilities to recognize the strategy used in the poster. To assess students' abilities to discover or ascertain the strategy used in the poster on their own, ask students to write, as in the following example:

The poster shown above was made during the First World War. What was the poster designed to do? Explain how you came to this conclusion.

CRITERIA for feedback or rubrics:

- Clear, appropriate statement of the main point.
- Appropriateness of evidence.
- Soundness of reasoning and clarity of explanation.

Assess students' answers on both the soundness of their conclusions and their use of evidence from the poster to support their conclusions. Again, base feedback or scoring on the criteria, as illustrated in Chapter 2.

Identifying rhetorical mechanisms is important to all subject areas. Students can be assessed on their understanding of any material that intends to persuade. Here is an example from English/language arts:

In *The Adventures of Tom Sawyer,* Tom is punished for playing hooky on Friday by being made to whitewash a fence on Saturday. He convinces his friends to help him and to pay him for the privilege. Reread the scene in the book in which he accomplishes this. Describe Tom's strategies for convincing his friends. If you were one of Tom's friends, would you have "fallen for" these strategies? Why or why not?

CRITERIA for feedback or rubrics:

- Clear, appropriate thesis evaluating Tom's strategies and the student's response.
- Appropriateness of evidence.
- Soundness of reasoning and clarity of explanation.

Assess students on the soundness of their description of Tom's tactics and their application of these strategies to their own personalities. Do not assess students on whether they would or would not have fallen for Tom's cunning, but on their analysis. Use feedback, rubrics, or a combination of both, depending on the purpose of your assessment.

And finally, the following is an example of identifying persuasive tactics in science. This example also requires judging the credibility of a source. Much of the persuasive evidence is from scientific studies and data analysis, and the credibility of the scientists and their methods is one of the important persuasive elements of the argument. This example also requires the ability to analyze arguments (see Chapter 3).

The U.S. Environmental Protection Agency (EPA) reports, "An 'unequivocal' warming trend of about 1.0 to 1.7°F occurred from 1906–2005. Warming occurred in both the Northern and Southern Hemispheres, and over the oceans." The EPA also reports that it is "very likely" that the warming trend will continue and that weather patterns will change as a result. This information can be found on the EPA Web site: www.epa.gov/climatechange/science/index.html.

In contrast, William Yeatman argues that many people's definitions and responses to global warming are "alarmist" and may in fact be counterproductive for society. This information can be found on the Web site Global-Warming.org: http://www.globalwarming.org/category/global-warming-101/.

Obviously, these two sources differ in their views on global warming. However, you will also see they differ in the ways in which they attempt to persuade their readers of their points of view. The Web sites differ in terms of purpose and audience, and therefore they use different strategies to accomplish their purposes and reach their audiences.

Compare and contrast the persuasive tactics used on each of these Web sites. Consider both the information given and how it is displayed on the Web pages. Use examples from the Web sites to support your discussion. What is your response to these tactics?

CRITERIA for feedback or rubrics:

- Clear, appropriate comparison of the rhetorical tactics used by the two Web sites regarding whether global warming is a real threat.
- Appropriateness of evidence.
- Soundness of reasoning and clarity of explanation.

Assess students on their identification and explanation of the communication tactics displayed on each Web site, on the soundness of students' comparison and contrast of the two, and on the clarity and completeness of students' discussion. If you use this as an extended written project, you could adapt the rubrics in Figure 3.3 (pp. 80–81).

Formative and Summative Uses of Results

The quality of student responses to the examples in this chapter of assessing students' critical and reasoned judgment, and to other similar assessments, depends on the soundness of their conclusion, thesis, or main judgment; on the relevance of the evidence they used to support their judgment; and on the logic they used to organize their evidence in support of their judgment.

For formative uses, give students feedback using these three criteria (thesis or conclusion, evidence, and reasoning). Check to make sure that students understand the feedback. Once they have received feedback that helps them see the reasoning that should support a conclusion, in effect the task becomes an assessment of recall for that student. For example, if your feedback helped explain to a student why and how the environmental Web sites differed, then if the student revised the assignment, he or she would be expressing comprehension of your feedback, not analysis and evaluation of the Web sites.

Therefore, after formative assessment, administer another assessment task requiring similar reasoning and see if students can use what they learned to do better on this question. For more in-depth reasoning practice, ask students then to explain the similarities in the old and new problems, and explain how they applied what they learned from feedback on the first one to their response on the second.

For summative uses, a rubric like the one in Figure 4.1 (p. 92) can be helpful. This general rubric might be adapted for use with specific tasks. As we have seen, rubrics can also be used formatively *if* they are used as vehicles for feedback and the obtained "score" is not used as part of a final grade.

Summing Up

The ability to use reasoned judgment and critical thinking is a hallmark of an educated person. And yet we often miss opportunities to teach and assess it directly or to associate it with subject area content. We might, for example, expect students to use sound judgment in resisting peer pressure to take drugs. This kind of judgment requires evaluating the credibility of a source, identifying peers' assumptions, and figuring out their persuasive tactics. It's easy to see the need for "judgment" in this social sense but sometimes harder to see it in an academic context.

In the next chapter, we turn to problem solving. Unlike judgment, problem solving is much touted in all academic disciplines. Like judgment, however, problem solving requires figuring something out. Both judgment or critical thinking and problem solving depend on students' abilities to make inferences from information they encounter.

5 | Assessing Problem Solving

Every subject has "problems" in the sense of goals that need to be reached, where the way to reach the goal is not automatic and requires thinking. While this book was in preparation, for example, economists and political leaders were trying to solve a big "problem": what combination of policies and strategies would have the most positive effect on jobs, money flow, and the stock market, to address the problem of a global recession. Not every problem is quite as complex and far-reaching as this one. However, this illustration shows that there are "problems" in every discipline.

What Is Problem Solving?

A good problem solver identifies exactly what the problem is, what might be obstacles to solving it, and what solutions might be expected to work. A good problem solver then tries at least one of the solutions. For more complex problems, a good problem solver can prioritize and evaluate the relative effectiveness of different solution strategies (Marzano et al., 1993). If a problem presents something so well known to a student that he or she can complete the task without having to reason, the student does not have to use problem-solving skills, and the scenario is not really a "problem" for that student.

Bransford and Stein (1984) classified problem-solving skills into a five-stage process called the IDEAL Problem Solver:

I   Identify the problem.
D Define and represent the problem.
E Explore possible strategies.
A Act on the strategies.
L Look back and evaluate the effects of your activities.

Bransford and Stein specifically organized the steps into an acronym to aid memory. In fact, using acronyms is one of the solution strategies students use when they are required to memorize information, *if* they first are able to define the assignment in terms of a problem. The problem is "How can I remember these things?" and the solution is "By using this acronym."

The IDEAL steps are easy to remember and helpful for both students and teachers. Students can use the IDEAL steps to work their way through problems. And for teachers, the IDEAL analysis can help focus in on one or more problem-solving tasks for instruction and assessment. For example, you can teach students how to identify problems and why that's important. Then you can specifically use assessment tasks that ask students to identify problems.

Many different rubrics for problem solving are widely available. I mentioned some of these in Chapter 1. The advantage of using a general problem-solving rubric is that students will come to see the types of thinking expected in the general rubric as learning goals. (By "general problem-solving rubric," I mean rubrics about problem-solving strategies, not task-specific rubrics that specify the answers to a particular problem.) With continued use, students will develop a concept about what constitutes good problem solving based on the rubrics they use. However, this also means that you should be careful to select rubrics that define problem solving in a way that is consistent with the problem solving you do in your subject with your students. For example, it will be hard to emphasize the importance of *defining* a problem if you use rubrics that do not mention or evaluate that aspect of problem solving.

In the following sections, I suggest ways to assess various aspects of the problem-solving process. For each multiple-choice problem, the choice of answer represents the student's thinking, and the scoring (right/wrong or 1/0) indicates that thinking. For constructed-response problems, you would provide either feedback or scoring (see Chapter 1), as appropriate to the skill the question was intended to assess, using the criteria given. For full-blown problems, a complete problem-solving rubric would be appropriate.

Different Kinds of Problems

Some exercises that are called "problems" do not require higher-order thinking and are not problems in the sense we are using the term here. For example, a science textbook might have a chapter on balancing chemical equations, with a set of problems at the end that all require manipulating the values such that the same number of atoms appear on each side of the equation in the simplest form. Each question has one right answer, and there are a very limited number of solution strategies, all of which are mathematically equivalent. The thinking required to do this kind of problem is comprehension of the concept of balance in a chemical equation and application of this principle to examples that are just like ones done in class or in the text. These are perfectly good "problems" or exercises, but they do not require higher-order thinking as we are using the term. In Bloom's terms, they are Apply-level problems. For the chemical equations example, the solution strategy is apparent and has usually been directly taught: multiply the molecules by values that result in the same number of atoms of each element on each side of the equation.

For problems that require higher-order thinking, the solution strategy *is not* immediately apparent. Problems that require higher-order thinking are *nonroutine* problems.

Structured Versus Unstructured Problems

Problems vary in the amount of *structure* you provide students. The more decisions that are open to the student, the less structured the problem. For example, a science teacher might ask students to build a terrarium that has a sustainable ecosystem, needing no additional water or food during a specified period of time. This is a very unstructured problem. Students would have to define the kind of ecosystem they wanted, identify the elements they would use for constructing it, obtain the elements, construct the terrarium, make regular observations to ensure that it was a sustainable ecosystem, and adjust the elements accordingly. Alternatively, the teacher might specify what kind of ecosystem with what elements, leaving students with a much more structured problem to solve: how to put the elements together and how to demonstrate sustainability.

Unstructured problems are more typical of real-life problems. Highly structured problems allow the teacher more control over the content of students' work. Teachers can use varying amounts of structure, but they should recognize what sort of problem they are using and make sure the problem requires the specific problem-solving skills they intend to assess.

"Goal-Free" Problems

Ayres (1993) did an experiment in which he asked high school students to solve geometry problems involving angles. He randomly assigned students to one of two versions of the problem set. The problems in each set were identical except for the end point. One group of students had conventional directions: "Find x," where x was the measure of a specific angle. Directions for the other group of students read: "Find all unknown angles." Ayres called these "goal-free" problems, but he meant "goal" in the sense of "one required answer" for the problem. Teachers would call these "unstructured" problems and would say they do have a student learning goal—understanding and using properties of angles in geometry.

You might think that the students in the group with the more open-ended problems would be less successful than the students with the more structured version of the problems. However, the opposite was the case. Students in the unstructured problem group were more successful than students in the conventional group. This result was consistent with Ayres's hypothesis. He reasoned that students who worked backward from a specific, desired end-state would use means-end analysis, in this case reasoning backward from the desired angle measure, identifying angle by angle which measures could be found that would lead to the solution. The unstructured group was free to just find angle measures, in any order, until they had completed the problem. Thus their cognitive load was less—and yet they learned more.

Assessing Problem Solving

To assess whether students can solve problems involving the particular content and concepts you are teaching, present students with a nonroutine scenario that requires either that they accomplish one of the IDEAL tasks (for instance, identify a problem, explore strategies, evaluate the most efficient solution) or use all the steps to do a full-blown problem-solving task. Examples of some assessments of problem solving are presented here.

Identify a Problem to Be Solved

Identifying or defining a problem is the first step toward solving it. This step is very much akin to the "focus on the question or main idea" kinds of tasks we discussed in Chapter 2. To assess problem identification, present a scenario or problem description and ask students to identify the problem that needs to be solved. Or present a statement that contains the problem and ask students to pose the question that needs to be answered in order to solve the problem. Students should express the questions in terms of the language and concepts of the subject you are teaching. Here is a mathematics problem for which identifying the problem is the most critical step to solving it.

This question requires you to show your work and explain your reasoning. You may use drawings, words, and numbers in your explanation. Your answer should be clear enough so that another person could read it and understand your thinking. It is important that you show all your work.

13. In a game, Carla and Maria are making subtraction problems using tiles numbered 1 to 5. The player whose subtraction problem gives the largest answer wins the game. Look at where each girl placed two of her tiles.

CARLA

| 1 | | |

| – | 5 | |

MARIA

| | | 5 |

| – | | 1 |

STILL TO PLACE:
2, 3, 4

STILL TO PLACE:
2, 3, 4

Who will win the game? _____
Explain how you know this person will win.

Source: National Assessment of Educational Progress, Mathematics, grade 8, Block 1996-8M3, no. 13. Available: http://nces.ed.gov/nationsreportcard/itmrlsx/landing.aspx

CRITERIA for feedback or rubrics:

- Identifies that Maria will win.
- Clear, logical explanation based on reasoning about place value.

The question, as written, asks for a complete solution. But the key to solving this problem is understanding what the problem is. It is a place-value problem. Identifying the location of the largest (5) and smallest (1) numbers in strategic places in the problem is the key to solving it. Carla has used her smallest number in the hundreds place of the top number (giving her the smallest possible potential starting values) and her largest in the tens place of the bottom number (giving her the largest possible numbers to take away).

Once the problem has been identified, the solution and explanation fall into place. Identifying the problem is a major part of solving this one. Assess students' explanations specifically for how they conceptualized the problem.

Identify Irrelevancies

Many real-life problems require students to figure out what information is important or relevant and what is not in order to identify and solve the problem. To assess how students identify what is and isn't relevant to a particular problem, present interpretive materials and a problem statement and ask students to identify all the irrelevant information.

Identifying irrelevancies can be simple and fairly concrete. For example, elementary mathematics students are taught to identify relevant and irrelevant information in word problems. Consider the following problem:

> Mr. Jones bought 12 cookies. He gave Deon 3 cookies and Tyrone 5 cookies. How many more cookies did Tyrone have than Deon?

Elementary students should learn to figure out that the fact that there were a dozen cookies in all is irrelevant to solving the problem, which involves subtracting three from five. Identifying irrelevant information is important to solving classroom-based academic problems. To see if students can identify the irrelevancy, you could ask them to solve the problem and explain their reasoning. You could also explicitly ask what information they would use and what information they would not use, and why.

An important "identifying irrelevancies" problem in all disciplines is how to search for information for an assignment. This problem is very difficult for some students, who head to the library or the Internet and simply "look up" everything they can find on the topic. To produce a good paper or project and distinguish relevant from irrelevant information, students need more than a topic. They need a research question, and they need to stay with it long enough to verify findings and draw concepts from the findings (Kuhlthau, 2005). Sometimes students looking up information for a paper or project get distracted by interesting but irrelevant information they run across along the way—or worse, they don't realize the information is irrelevant. We have all read term papers that are "dumps" of everything found in the library, without any sense of what is relevant and what isn't.

A strategy to avoid this "topic dumping" is to make students first choose a topic and then write a question about it. So, for instance, a high school English student may choose to do a term paper about Shakespeare, which is a fine topic. But imagine what would happen if she went to the library and the Internet with the mission "to find out about Shakespeare"! The result would be an overwhelming and unfocused bunch of information, and the student would have no criteria or strategy for figuring out what information was relevant for her.

If the student writes a research question about the topic, however, the question can serve as part of her problem-solving strategy. She will find that some preliminary reading about Shakespeare is useful, showing her what's available and perhaps giving her some ideas. But fairly early in the project, she needs to write an actual question to investigate, perhaps one such as this: "Where did Shakespeare get the ideas for his plays?" Information that helps answer that question is relevant. Other information, however interesting, is not.

McClymer and Knoles (1992) observed that students without the skill of knowing what is relevant and what is not *cope* with assignments rather than *learning* from them. Two of these coping mechanisms involve students' producing what McClymer and Knoles called "clumps" or "shapes." *Clumps* are clods of information shoveled up without underlying logic or explanation. Students can clump data, reproducing lots of information with little or no thinking; they can clump jargon, using technical language without really understanding it; and they can clump assertions, for example by making thesis statements surrounded by lots of "stuff" that doesn't really support the thesis.

Shapes are arguments in the right form but without substance. Some common shapes students employ to mimic critical thinking without actually doing it include borrowing the analysis of another author, analyzing only surface meanings, and analyzing a single thread or issue as if it represented the topic. A colleague of mine calls this "having the words without the music."

Students who clump lack the critical-thinking skills listed here as being able to "focus on a question" and "identify irrelevancies." Students who cannot do these things are often overwhelmed by assignments. An information technology specialist who works in a university library tells me that secondary teachers often ask him what they should teach their students about new information technologies to help them prepare for college. The teachers usually are think-ing about things like how to use electronic card catalogs, how to find journal articles online, and the like.

My librarian friend always says no, technology isn't the issue teachers should worry about. He says what secondary teachers should do is teach their students how to ask questions and how to judge what information is relevant to answering the question and what isn't. If you can just teach them that, he says, your students will be fine. A librarian can demonstrate computer applications to students as needed. But when students go to the library with the agenda "to look up" something (for instance, "to look up the American Revolution" or "to look up the circulatory system"), without knowing what information will be relevant to their assignment and what won't, they're doomed.

To assess whether students can identify irrelevancies to a larger prob-lem like what information should go into a paper or thesis, I recommend an assignment that proceeds in stages. First, ask students to pick topics and read enough on their topic so that they can write a single sentence, either a research question or a thesis statement. Help students evaluate the usefulness of these questions or theses. Is the question important in the discipline? Is enough relevant information likely to be available? This formative assessment should help students make their final products better.

Once the question itself has been settled, students can locate information and prepare a brief essay or an outline, organizing their work to date. You and the student can assess how the project or paper is progressing. Is the infor-mation listed relevant to the question or thesis, and can the student explain how? Finally, after these opportunities for formative and corrective feedback, students can proceed to finish the project or paper. Scoring of the final project should include an appraisal of how well the students have put together infor-mation to answer their research question or support their thesis. The rubrics in Figure 3.3 (pp. 80–81) are one way of doing this.

Describe and Evaluate Multiple Strategies

Describing several different strategies that could be used to solve a prob-lem is a real-world skill. Prioritizing the strategies according to criteria that are important for the specific problem (for example, the most efficient, most effective, least expensive, and so on), either before trying them or after trying several of them, and deciding which is the best strategy, is also an important higher-order thinking skill.

To assess how students describe multiple problem-solving strategies, state a problem and ask students to solve the problem in two or more ways and show their solutions using pictures, diagrams, or graphs. Or state a problem and two or more acceptable strategies for solving it, and ask students to explain why both strategies are correct. In writing an item you might, for example, state that these were different ways that two fictional students solved the problem. Consider these examples:

Amanda and her friends have noticed a problem in their neighborhood. The garbage cans in the public park are overflowing.

Scenario source: National Assessment of Educational Progress, Civics, grade 8, Block 2006-8C6, no. 13. Available: http://nces.ed.gov/nationsreportcard/itmrlsx/landing.aspx

1.   Name at least two things Amanda and her friends could do on their own to help solve this problem. Which one would you recommend they try first? Explain why.

2.   Name at least two things local government could do to help solve this problem. Which one would you recommend they try first? Explain why.

CRITERIA for feedback or rubrics for Question 1:

- Identification and prioritization of two reasonable methods available to private citizens.
- Appropriateness of evidence.
- Soundness of reasoning and clarity of explanation.

CRITERIA for feedback or rubrics for Question 2:

- Identification and prioritization of two reasonable methods available to local government.
- Appropriateness of evidence.
- Soundness of reasoning and clarity of explanation.

These questions assess both problem-solving skills and content knowledge. Students would need to know about the resources and methods available to private citizens and local governments. They would need to have an appreciation of the amount of time, energy, and money required for civil and government actions. Knowledge of similar events that happened in the past would also help.

Any problem for which students have brainstormed multiple solutions lends itself to evaluating the quality of those solutions. You can assess how students evaluate the quality of a solution in several ways. One way is to ask students to produce several different solutions. Another way is to provide several solutions to students and ask them to evaluate those solutions. If you provide solutions to evaluate, be certain to vary their correctness and quality, so that students can display their ability to evaluate. For example, some may be more efficient, some may have negative consequences, and some may not work at all. Assess the students' ability to appraise and describe the quality of each of the strategies.

In addition to problems with multiple-solution strategies, sometimes problems can have multiple good solutions. Here is a mathematics example that asks students to generate two different solutions to a problem.

Question 6 refers to the situation described below.

A school yard contains only bicycles and wagons like those in the figure above.

6. On Tuesday the total number of wheels in the school yard was 24. There are several ways this could happen.

    a. How many bicycles and how many wagons could there be for this to happen?

    Number of bicycles _____
    Number of wagons _____

    b. Find another way that this could happen.

    Number of bicycles _____
    Number of wagons _____

Source: National Assessment of Educational Progress, Mathematics, grade 4, Block 2003-4M7, no. 6. Available: http://nces.ed.gov/nationsreportcard/itmrlsx/landing.aspx

More information about students' problem-solving skills could be obtained if you asked students to show their work and explain their reasoning for the solution. Evaluate the explanations using a rubric or feedback that focuses on the clarity, completeness, and appropriateness of the reasoning.

For a more in-depth look at students' uses of multiple strategies to solve problems, consider using a performance assessment. For example, here is a performance assessment task in elementary school science. It assesses classification skills (also a mathematics learning target), reasoning, and employing multiple strategies for solution. It helps students understand the idea that multiple classification systems can exist, and some are more helpful than others.

Over the course of a week, have children bring in as many different leaves as they can find in their neighborhood. At the end of the week, divide the leaves into piles—as many piles as there would be groups of four students in the class. Each group is given a pile of leaves and the following tasks:

continued

1. Observe each leaf and talk about it with your group. Describe each leaf in as many different ways as you can (shape, size, and so on). Then sort the leaves into smaller piles based on ways they are alike. Groups should discuss the descriptions until everyone understands, and then everyone should write their own notes. After the sorting, each person should write down how many piles there are, what kind of leaves are in each pile, and why you sorted the leaves this way.

2. Now sort the leaves again, in another way. Again, each person should write down how many piles there are, what kind of leaves are in each pile, and why you sorted the leaves this way.

3. You can make as many different sorting schemes as you want, but you should have at least two. For each different sorting strategy you use, each person should write down how many piles there are, what kind of leaves are in each pile, and why you sorted the leaves this way.

At this point, assess the groups of four on their group cooperation skills and the quality of their content-related discussion. You can do this by giving formative feedback and by asking group members to give feedback to each other briefly. Then ask students to individually complete the following tasks, using the notes they took during the group work:

4. Describe how your group sorted the leaves. How many different ways did you find to do that? How many different piles did you make each time, and why did you make them? You can use words and pictures to explain your thinking.

Assess this individual portion of the problem solving with a science problem-solving rubric that includes criteria for thinking and reasoning as well as for content. Assess content not on whether the students settled on a standard scientific classification, but on whether the answer communicated understanding that observing and organizing natural phenomena (like leaves) could be useful, and why. Notice that this performance assessment is based on group work but assesses individual understanding. Group work skills are assessed during the group work. Also note that you would not do a performance assessment with a group component like this unless you had taught your students how to do group work.

5. Which way of sorting the leaves do you think would be most useful? Explain why you think that.

CRITERIA for feedback or rubrics:

- Clear, appropriate description of each classification scheme.
- Clear statement about which classification scheme is most useful.
- Appropriateness of evidence.
- Soundness of reasoning and clarity of explanation.

Model a Problem

The following anecdote clearly illustrates how important it is to be able to wrap one's head around the nature of a problem in order to solve it with thinking, not with plugging numbers into a formula by rote:

A colleague of ours teaches an introductory calculus section. Early one term, he and his class were working through some standard motion problems: "A boy drops a water balloon from a window. If it takes 0.8 seconds to strike his erstwhile friend, who is 5 feet tall, how high is the window?" On the exam, the problem took this form: "Someone walking along the edge of a pit accidentally kicks into it a small stone, which falls to the bottom in 2.3 seconds. How deep is the pit?" One student was visibly upset. The question was not fair, she protested. The instructor had promised that there would not be any material on the exam that they had not gone over in class. "But we did a dozen of those problems in class," our colleague said. "Oh no," shot back the student, "we never did a single pit problem." (McClymer & Knoles, 1992, p. 33)

During instruction, this student had applied solution strategies by rote to problems she did not understand. She had not grasped the concept of a "motion problem" involving the relationships among distance, time, velocity, and acceleration, and was not able to identify this problem as a motion problem. The instructor had encouraged his students to draw the problems each time, which this student had not done during her studies. Those drawings would have served as models of motion problems. Thus although this is a sad story, the exam yielded valid information. The student did not understand motion problems.

To assess how students model a problem, state a problem and ask students to draw a diagram or picture showing the problem situation. Assess students on how well they represent the problem rather than on whether the problem is correctly solved. Drawings of time problems in mathematics, for example, should depict time lines, not scales. Drawings of motion problems should depict motion. The instructor in the calculus example could have assessed, rather than just encouraged, students' drawings of the motion problems as part of his formative assessment. In prior classroom assessments and on the exam, students could have been asked to include their drawings in their work and explain their meaning. Students and instructor would have gained information specifically about how each student modeled the problems.

Identify Obstacles or Additional Information for Solving a Problem or Scenario

Solving problems well is sometimes as much about figuring out the right information to use as it is about inventing a solution. To assess how students identify obstacles and decide whether additional information is needed for solving a problem, present a complex problem to solve and ask students to explain why it is difficult to complete the task, what the obstacle or obstacles are, and what additional information they need. Assess whether students can identify the obstacle to solving the problem. Here is an example:

Teresia is a small country that has been invaded by its neighbor Corollia. The king of Teresia is a long-standing United States ally who has been living in exile since the Corollian invasion. Teresia is an important exporter of uranium; it sends most of its supply to members of the European Union. The king appeals to the United States and the United Nations for military help in driving Corollia from his country.

12. What official argument would members of the United Nations be most likely to make for supporting military efforts against Corollia?

    A. The stability of the international system depends on countries maintaining their current forms of government.

    B. The United Nations and the European Union should control the mining of uranium worldwide.

    *C. The stability of the international system depends on absolute respect for national borders and sovereignty.

    D. Countries such as the United States should become the main judges in all international disputes.

13. Identify two pieces of information not given above that you would need before you could decide whether or not the United States military should help Teresia. Explain why each piece of information would be important.

Source: National Assessment of Educational Progress, Civics, grade 8, Block 2006-8C4, nos. 12–13. Available: http://nces.ed.gov/nationsreportcard/itmrlsx/landing.aspx

CRITERIA for feedback or rubrics:

- Clear, appropriate identification of two additional pieces of information.
- Appropriateness of evidence.
- Soundness of reasoning and clarity of explanation.

This is an excellent example of assessing problem solving—specifically, identifying obstacles and needed information—in the context of a discipline. To identify the likely official UN argument (Question 12), a student would need to understand the mission of the United Nations and apply that understanding to the scenario. To identify additional needed information related to a United States decision about military aid (Question 13), a student requires additional content knowledge, for example the relationship of the U.S. military with the U.S. government and with society. For Question 13, students also must have the problem-solving skill of identifying what additional information is needed to put all that together in an argument for military intervention.

To illustrate once more how the criteria can be used as the basis of simple rubrics for brief essay questions, here is an example of how you could use the criteria to make a holistic, 2-1-0 rubric for Question 13. The levels could also be called 3-2-1, or 4-2-0, or 5-3-1, depending on your scoring and grading needs. As before, to make a holistic rubric, describe quality on each of the criteria for each level.

Does the student reason about the problem to arrive at a clear identification of two pieces of information that the United States would need before deciding on military aid to Teresia?

 2 = Completely and clearly—Response gives a clear, appropriate identification of two additional pieces of information. Reasoning is sound and includes appropriate evidence about U.S. policies. Explanation is clear.

 1 = Partially—Response identifies two additional pieces of information. Some reasoning is sound and includes some evidence about U.S. policies. Some of the explanation is not clear or is only partial.

 0 = No—Response does not identify two additional pieces of information. Reasoning is not sound or does not include evidence about U.S. policies. Explanation is not clear or is missing.

For more in-depth assessment of students' abilities to identify and use additional information, consider using a performance assessment. In the Teresia and Corollia example, for instance, you might expand the question to ask students to identify at least two additional pieces of information the United States should have before deciding whether to send military aid to Teresia. Ask students to explain their reasoning and use evidence from other similar requests for U.S. military aid in recent U.S. history, using the library and other resources. What information was persuasive in the decision to send troops (or not) in those cases, and how does that relate to this scenario? As with the previous performance assessments, build in formative assessment opportunities at various stages of the project. At the end, grade the project with an adapted version of the rubrics in Figure 3.3 (pp. 80–81). Make sure to give students a copy of the rubrics before they begin. Have students discuss the criteria and apply them to examples of student work to help them more fully understand the qualities on which their thinking will be assessed.

Reason with Data

To assess how students reason with data, present interpretive material (story, cartoon, graph, data table) and a problem that requires using information from the material. Then ask students to solve the problem and explain the procedure they used to reach a solution. On the following page is a social studies example that requires students to draw a conclusion from a graph. Graph-reading skills and quantitative reasoning, often thought of as mathematical skills, are required, but the interpretation is a civics issue. Reasoning with data often requires this kind of cross-disciplinary thinking.

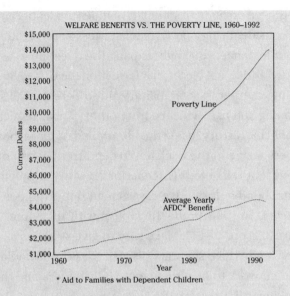

WELFARE BENEFITS VS. THE POVERTY LINE, 1960–1992

* Aid to Families with Dependent Children

16. Which of the following statements is supported by the data presented in the graph above?

    A. In current dollars the poverty line has decreased substantially in the thirty years following 1960.

    B. The average yearly AFDC benefits increased substantially during the Bush presidency, 1989–1992.

    C. In current dollars the average AFDC benefit remained constant over the period covered by the graph.

  *D. Since about 1980, the average annual benefit of a family receiving AFDC has declined relative to the poverty line.

Source: National Assessment of Educational Progress, Civics, grade 12, Block 2006-12C7, no. 16. Available: http://nces.ed.gov/nationsreportcard/itmrlsx/landing.aspx

And here is an elementary science example. To solve this problem, students would have to combine two kinds of information from the table: whether there was precipitation, and whether it was cold enough to snow.

The table below shows information about the weather in four cities on the same day.

	City 1	City 2	City 3	City 4
High Temperature	65° F	80° F	48° F	25° F
Low Temperature	56° F	66° F	38° F	10° F
Precipitation—Rain or Snow (Inches)	2 inches	0 inches	1 inch	1 inch

8. In which city did snow most likely fall at some time during the day?

   A. City 1
   B. City 2
   C. City 3
   *D. City 4

Source: National Assessment of Educational Progress, Science, grade 4, Block 2005-4S12, no. 8. Available: http://nces.ed.gov/nationsreportcard/itmrlsx/landing.aspx

Both of these problems involve reasoning with data, but each has one right answer. It is possible, and often desirable, to write more open-ended performance assessment tasks that require reasoning with data. For example, you might give students the AFDC graph and ask them to describe two or more conclusions they could draw from it, and explain their reasoning. Or you might ask them to describe two or more conclusions, and brainstorm what additional information they might want in order to explore possible causes for the decline of AFDC benefits relative to the poverty line, or reasons for the sharp increase in the poverty line.

You might also pose a task for students requiring them to collect and analyze their own data from which they then draw conclusions. Science lab experiments often do this. Here is an example from consumer science:

Keep a food diary for a week. Write down everything you eat and drink at each meal and for snacks. Then make a bar graph to show how many servings per day, on average, you have eaten of grains, vegetables, fruits, oils, milk, and meat and beans. These are the categories from the U.S. Department of Agriculture's Food Pyramid (www.mypyramid.gov). If you have consumed anything that does not fit these categories, you may need to add a category or two to your bar graph. (For example, candy is not a food group!) After you have prepared your graph, write a brief essay interpreting what it means.

What conclusions can you draw from your graph? How well does your eating follow the USDA recommendations? What have you learned from analyzing your own eating pattern for a week? Explain your reasoning.

CRITERIA for feedback or rubrics:

- Accuracy and completeness of student data.
- Clear thesis about what student learned about his or her own eating habits.
- Appropriateness of evidence.
- Soundness of reasoning and clarity of explanation.

Performance assessments requiring students to collect and analyze their own data, from which they then draw conclusions, can be done at all grade levels. For example, you could ask elementary school students to find out about the number of siblings or number and kind of pets among their classmates. You could ask middle or high school social studies classes to poll family and friends about election results or local issues. Any of these could form the basis of a performance assessment of the ability to reason with data.

Use Analogies

We discussed reasoning by analogy in Chapter 3. It is sometimes useful in problem solving. Analogical reasoning allows students to apply a solution strategy for one problem to solve another problem that is similar. The key is that the similarities between the two situations have to be on attributes that are relevant to the problem and its solution.

To assess how students use analogies, present a problem statement and a correct solution strategy, and ask students to describe other problems that could (by analogy) be solved by using this same solution strategy and explain why the solution to the problem they generated is like the solution to the problem you gave them. Assess the analogical relationship of the students' solution strategy to the strategy you gave them. Here is an example:

Members of a certain congressional committee talked a lot during committee hearings. Some members talked to explain their own views, some treated a witness as hostile and tried to discredit that witness's testimony, some wanted to prevent their opponents on the committee from speaking, and some wanted to prolong the debate and the hearing to postpone or prolong a committee vote. To solve this problem, rules were established to give each committee member a fixed amount of time to speak and to ask questions of a witness. Under these rules, a committee member is allowed to give another member all or part of his allotted time.

1. Describe several other problems in different situations that could be solved by using a set of rules similar to those that the congressional committee used.

2. For each of the problems you listed, explain how the rules might be modified and why this would solve the problem you listed.

Source: From *Educational Assessment of Students* (5th ed., p. 220), by A. J. Nitko & S. M. Brookhart, 2007, Upper Saddle River, NJ: Pearson Education.

continued

CRITERIA for feedback or rubrics:

- For each analogous situation listed, a clear, appropriate thesis about how similar rules could apply in that situation, with appropriate modifications.
- Appropriateness of evidence.
- Soundness of reasoning and clarity of explanation.

Whether you give formative feedback or score the results for summative purposes, assess both the quality of students' reasoning from one situation to the other and the quality of the application of the solution from one situation to the other. Students should be able to explain the similarities in the problem situations and how those similarities are relevant to the problem solution.

Solve a Problem Backward

Solving a problem backward requires what cognitive psychologists call "means-end analysis" (Ayres, 1993). Students need to figure out ways to successively reduce the differences between the problem as presented and the desired solution. Solving a problem backward can be a good learning strategy for some kinds of closed problems, which is one reason that many textbooks print answers to exercises at the back of the book. Students can work backward from the answer and see how to solve the problem. Eventually, they can tackle similar problems without first looking up the answer.

To assess how students solve more open problems backward, present a complex problem situation or a complex, multistep task to complete. Ask students to work backward from the desired outcome to develop a plan or a strategy for completing the task or solving the problem.

For example, in all content areas students do research papers or complex projects that require planning. The problem is easy enough to identify: "How can I arrange my work so that I end up with a good-quality, completed project by the due date?" Reasoning backward, students can plan the steps and time frame needed to complete the project or paper. They might record these plans on planning sheets or as to-do lists. You can add structure to the problem, for example by providing planning-sheet templates, or leave it less structured, requiring students to come up with their own planning methods. Here is a consumer science example of reasoning backward to solve a problem:

You are having 10 people over to your house for dinner at 6:00 p.m. tomorrow night, and you want to serve an entrée and a dessert. You will arrive home from school at 4:00 p.m. tomorrow. You have two pounds of ground beef on hand that you would like to use, and you have time to stop at the store on the way home from school today.

1. Identify the recipes you will fix for dinner tomorrow and plan when you will start preparing each dish.

2. Make a shopping list for your stop at the store this afternoon.

CRITERIA for feedback or rubrics:

- Clear, appropriate solution including
   - feasible recipes given the constraints of the problem and
   - reasonable shopping and cooking plans.
- Soundness of reasoning and clarity of explanation.

In this problem, part of the end state—dinner tomorrow at 6:00 p.m.—is specified. Students need to apply reasoning as well as content knowledge to figure out the rest of the end state (what particular dishes to serve). Students need to reason backward to solve the rest of the problem so they have the right ingredients and enough preparation time for the dishes they selected.

Formative and Summative Uses of Results

Any of the examples in this chapter could be used formatively or summatively. For each example, I listed criteria on which students would be assessed.

Formative assessment would base feedback on the criteria, with descriptive comments and observations about the work and suggestions for improvement. Small rubrics, like the 2-1-0 variety (or longer as needed), would use the same criteria on a scale, and I have given some examples of this. Larger assessments would have larger rubrics, because you should be able to make more distinctions in quality with more evidence. I have varied the examples for the sake of readability, sometimes giving rubrics and sometimes not, but always giving the criteria. Criteria are the building blocks of formative or summative assessment. You will not likely be using these assessment examples as is, anyway. They are examples of how you would work in your own content area and grade level. The point here is that you always prepare criteria and plans for using them, whether in feedback, scoring rubrics, or both, when you plan an assessment.

Formative assessment of problem solving begins in classrooms where student reasoning is made explicit, "think-aloud" fashion, and where discussing the reasoning behind problem solutions is a routine activity. Fishbowling, brainstorming, and other classroom activities that allow multiple-solution strategies to be generated and discussed can help.

For both formative and summative assessment, problem-solving rubrics can be useful for organizing students' thinking. Try to use general problem-solving rubrics, not task-specific ones, so that the students internalize as their goal the general strategies of identifying the problem, defining and representing the problem, exploring possible strategies, acting on the strategies, and looking back and evaluating the effects of the strategies. Using the same rubrics over and over again will help the students focus on the qualities described in those rubrics as their goal for successful problem solving.

Summing Up

Problem solving is important for all academic disciplines and for life. Ill-structured, open-ended problems require more student input and are more like real-life problems than well-structured problems. You can assess problem solving as a whole with a carefully designed problem and a problem-solving rubric. Or you can assess how students handle the stages of problem solving.

We discussed how to assess identifying a problem, defining and representing it, exploring and comparing solution strategies, using the strategies, and evaluating the results. Bransford and Stein (1984) call these stages "the IDEAL Problem Solver" and point out that both learning and creative thinking use these stages.

We turn next to how to assess creative thinking. This may seem like a contradiction, since assessment implies known criteria and creativity implies a venture into the unknown. Chapter 6 explains how assessment and creativity are not mutually exclusive. In fact, good assessment can support creative thinking. I have left this chapter until the end because creativity is probably the most poorly assessed and least understood higher-order thinking skill. Now that you have thought through other aspects of higher-order thinking, it should be easier to see how creativity fits with them.

6 | Assessing Creativity and Creative Thinking

Creativity is certainly something that teachers want to encourage in their students. And yet it's one of the most poorly handled aspects of classroom assessment. Many teachers want their students to be creative but are not entirely sure what to look for. For some classroom projects, teachers allot points to creativity but leave it undefined. Too often, creativity ends up meaning the report cover was nicely colored or something like that. Even worse, the "creativity" slot can end up being used as a "fudge factor" for the teacher's overall impression of the student. Creativity is not, as a colleague once railed, "cute animals with long eyelashes." But if creativity does not mean aesthetically pleasing or cute, what does it mean? How do you ask for it, and how do you know it when you see it?

What Is Creativity or Creative Thinking?

Creativity as this chapter will use the term means putting things together in new ways (either conceptually or artistically), observing things others might miss, constructing something novel, using unusual or unconventional imagery that nevertheless works to make an interesting point, and the like. This kind of thinking, and the product that it brings into being, can certainly include artistic creativity, but is not limited to it.

The way I like to think about this is that *learning* is when *you* have an "aha!" moment and things gel in your mind. *Creativity* is when you put things together so that *others* will have an "aha!" moment when considering your creation ("I never thought about it like that before").

Some theorists reserve the term *creativity* for generating original ideas, and separate creativity from the critical thinking that follows as students decide whether they are satisfied with their creation. Other theorists see these both as part of creative thinking.

Creative Thinking as Generative but Not Evaluative

One point of view about creativity holds that creative thinking is the brainstorming or putting together of new ideas, and then critical thinking takes over and evaluates how successful the new ideas are. Norris and Ennis (1989) are proponents of that view. Both critical and creative thinking, they argue, are important parts of good thinking. Both are often present in a real-life episode of good thinking. For example, creative thinking may result in a brainstormed list of possible activities, and critical thinking is needed to prioritize them and evaluate which one would be the best thing to do.

Norris and Ennis point out that, in general, thinking can be described according to whether it is reasonable or unreasonable, productive or nonproductive, reflective or nonreflective, and evaluative or nonevaluative. Using these characteristics, they distinguish the similarities of and differences between critical thinking and creative thinking. Creative thinking is reasonable, productive, and nonevaluative. Critical thinking is reasonable, reflective, and evaluative.

Reason. Both critical and creative thinking are reasonable. Unreasonable thinking, of any sort, is not good thinking.

Productivity. All creative thinking is productive. Whether the product is conceptual (such as a list of tentative hypotheses) or physical (such as a painting), something is created. Critical thinking does not always result in some sort of product, although it can. Creative thinking and critical thinking overlap when both production and reflection are needed, as, for example, when a student needs to brainstorm a list of possible hypotheses for a science experiment and then prioritize them for testing.

Reflectivity. All critical thinking is reflective, in the sense of engaging intentional thought. Some creative thinking is reflective: "Would I rather have this character go to the store or go to the movies in my next scene?" Some creative thinking, however, is nonreflective. We have various names for nonreflective creativity—intuition, inspiration, and such—and we admire it when it happens, as when a musical theme "just comes" to a composer. Some creativity is a mixture of reflective and nonreflective thinking. Our music composer may have an inspiration for a snippet of melody and use knowledge of music theory to craft that snippet into a theme for a composition.

Evaluation. According to Norris and Ennis, creative thinking is nonevaluative. In other words, *creative* thinking means "coming up with stuff," and *critical* thinking means evaluating what the stuff is good for.

So in most school assignments, creative and critical thinking go hand in hand in work that would be categorized at the Create level of Bloom's taxonomy. Students come up with responses to your assignments, and they also present them to you as finished work, presumably after exercising some critical judgment as to whether their response (project, essay, poem, term paper) fulfills the assignment's requirements and shows what they can do. As you assess students' creativity, you yourself are using critical judgment.

Creative Thinking as Both Generative and Evaluative

Not everyone would agree with Norris and Ennis's distinction between the generative (creative thinking) and evaluative (critical thinking) aspects of creativity. Creativity expert Sir Ken Robinson, for example, defines creativity as "a process of having original ideas that have value" (Azzam, 2009, p. 22). Robinson includes the evaluation of the idea—when the creator decides whether the new idea has value or not—as part of creativity. He points out that people are creative within disciplines, and each discipline has criteria for what is valuable and good.

So, for example, John Donne wrote original sonnets demonstrating great creativity. But these creations used a particular poetic form (sonnet form). Donne's poems also met other poetic criteria, like whether the imagery was evocative, how the words sounded, and so on. Without this disciplinary knowledge, Donne would not have created such elegant poems.

Or, for another example, Alexander Fleming created penicillin from the *penicillium notatum* mold after he discovered the mold seemed to be responsible for killing staphylococcus bacteria in a Petri dish. But he already was an expert scientist, with deep knowledge about bacteria, diseases, and lab procedures. Without such disciplinary knowledge, he would not have made the breakthrough.

Sweller (2009) also sees both the generation of ideas or products and testing them for effectiveness as aspects of creativity. He points out that some novelty can be achieved by just reorganizing ideas that already exist in new ways. Much of the creativity students exhibit in classrooms is this kind of creativity. He shows, however, that this kind of creativity requires a knowledge base from which to draw. Students can't reorganize ideas about characters in literature, or weather patterns in science, or political coups in history, or functions in mathematics unless they have a store of knowledge about these things. Additionally, Sweller points out that humans sometimes try truly new, "random" ideas—for example, in order to solve a problem for which they either do not have the relevant knowledge base from which to reason and prioritize solutions (so they cast about for pretty much anything), or for which such knowledge does not exist (as when cutting-edge researchers solve new problems).

A Middle Way: Attention to Both Generating and Evaluating

The Partnership for 21st Century Skills (www.p21.org) offers a compromise position on the question of whether creativity involves just the having of new ideas and the production of new creations or whether it also includes evaluating the value or worth of those ideas against disciplinary, social, or other standards. The Partnership (2009) groups student outcomes into four categories: Core Subjects and 21st Century Themes; Learning and Innovation Skills; Information, Media, and Technology Skills; and Life and Career Skills. The Learning and Innovation Skills category includes three subcategories: Creativity and Innovation, Critical Thinking and Problem Solving, and Communication and Collaboration.

Listing creativity and critical thinking as separate subcategories suggests the Partnership recognizes the distinction between the two, as do Norris and Ennis.

However, one of the points under Creativity and Innovation outcomes reads: "Elaborate, refine, analyze and evaluate their own ideas in order to improve and maximize creative efforts" (2009, p. 3). This suggests that innovation and evaluation go hand in hand. Whether discussed as part of the creative act or as reflection after it, critical thinking is necessary. With this I believe all the authors would agree. In this book, that's the position we'll take: one can discuss creativity and evaluation of the results of creativity separately, but in the end they are done together.

What Is Required for Creativity?

Before you can assess creativity, you have to be able to share what it is with students. If a student asked you what to do to improve his or her thinking, you would know what to say about analysis, synthesis, evaluation, logic and reasoning, critical judgment, and problem solving. But how does one get better at creativity? Just what is it that a student should "do" to be creative?

The following list of bullets is an attempt to put into operation what creative students actually do and is based on ideas from several sources. Robinson (Azzam, 2009) notes that creativity feeds on collaboration and diversity, which emphasizes the importance of having multiple sources of ideas. Sweller (2009) notes that idea generation, reorganization of ideas, trial and error, and a deep knowledge base are required for creativity. He emphasizes the importance both of having new ideas and of using different organizational methods to combine and process the ideas. The Partnership for 21st Century Skills (2009) also lists the kinds of actions students do when they think creatively, work creatively with others, and implement innovations. Joining these sources of information together, we can say that creative students do the following:

• Recognize the importance of a deep knowledge base and continually work to learn new things.

• Are open to new ideas and actively seek them out.

• Find "source material" for ideas in a wide variety of media, people, and events.

- Look for ways to organize and reorganize ideas into different categories and combinations, and then evaluate whether the results are interesting, new, or helpful.

- Use trial and error when they are not sure of how to proceed, viewing failure as an opportunity to learn.

Creative Problem Solving

A particularly interesting kind of creativity occurs when students define problems in new ways. In popular jargon, this is called "thinking outside the box." It is valued in school and in life, and it's one of the methods by which civilization advances. Creative problem solving involves identifying a problem with fresh eyes. The problem may end up being about something completely different than originally thought. Solving the "new" problem solves the old one, too. Here are two examples of creative problem solving.

An old example: The elevator story. I can't remember where I heard this story; I hope it's true! In the early 20th century, skyscrapers were a fairly new phenomenon. Skyscrapers only became possible after safe commercial elevator technology became available, because skyscrapers are too tall for people to be able to routinely take the stairs.

In one office building, a problem arose. People became annoyed and impatient waiting for the elevator to arrive. Grouchy employees felt their time was being wasted. The building owners called in the engineers and asked them to solve the problem of making the elevators faster. But they couldn't do that; the elevators were already traveling as fast as was safe.

An employee of the company solved the problem by redefining it. The problem wasn't that the elevators were too slow, it was that people *thought* they were too slow and got bored waiting for the elevator. The employee suggested installing mirrors by the elevator so that people had something else to do while they were waiting. Instead of "waiting," people checked their ties, hair, or makeup. They were no longer bored or impatient, and the time passed quickly.

A new example: Folds and wrinkles. As I was writing this book, I heard an interview on National Public Radio (NPR) with Lakshminarayanan Mahade-van, a mathematics professor at Harvard who had just been named a 2009

MacArthur Foundation fellow. This prize is nicknamed the "genius grant," and each awardee gets half a million dollars to use any way he or she wishes. Mahadevan applies mathematical theory to questions about nonlinear but common physical and biological events. How does cloth fold and drape? How does skin wrinkle? How do flags flutter?

In the interview, Mahadevan said he tries to explain common observations with mathematical theory. For example, he explained how he and his colleagues studied flowers blooming, using time-lapse photography and then explaining the observations. They found that petals grow along the edge more than they grow in the center. "So we made a mathematical theory for it," he says. "We tried to essentially connect that to experiments and empirical observations in the laboratory, which are easy to do, because you go to a florist and you buy half a dozen lilies, and you just watch them" (NPR, 2009).

In other words, Mahadevan looks at what might seem like normal, nonproblematic events, and wonders about them. He also hopes to be able to pass along his knack for problem finding to others. Asked how the grant would change his life, he said he didn't know because he was still in shock. "I certainly hope, and I know that it will, give me the kind of freedom that I've had—and even more now—to pursue problems which people didn't even think were problems. But also, I think, at a different level, maybe, to try and see if I can use this to try and encourage and inculcate curiosity in young people about everyday things" (NPR, 2009).

How Do You Promote Creativity in the Classroom?

Many common classroom activities and procedures foster students' creative work. Mathematics teachers, for example, sometimes teach students to use "guess and check" as a strategy for problem solving. The process of generating the guesses and then evaluating how close their guesses got to solving the problem encompasses both the "create" and "critique" aspects of creativity discussed previously.

Brainstorming, in any subject, is a classic creative activity. In a typical brainstorming session, all ideas are accepted and listed. Evaluation of the ideas comes later. This approach has the effect of generating a maximum number of ideas. It also exposes all students in the group to everyone's ideas, which can help stretch students' thinking and help them see how being open to ideas from others is useful.

Writing reader-response logs in reading or literature classes is a creative activity for students. In a typical reader-response log, students are asked to describe their thoughts, feelings, surprises, and other reactions after reading a text or selection. There are many ways to respond to literature, and students have an opportunity to connect elements of their own lives with those in the text—a "reorganizing" activity that can generate new insights.

Can You Grade Creativity?

Whether or not you can grade creativity depends on where you stand in the debate noted earlier about whether "creativity" is just the generative, productive act—saving "critique" to be a separate act—or whether creativity also includes critiquing the created product against criteria in a discipline. If you believe the former, creativity should be assessed and described with feedback: "Using an image of Hamlet on your poster for Mental Health Week was very creative. I have never seen anyone make a connection like that!" Simple generation of something new should, in my opinion, not be graded or scored in a rubric that ends up in a final grade. The act of grading itself is a kind of critique or evaluation. Azzam (2009) quotes Sir Ken Robinson as saying the following:

> Whether there should be an individual grade for creativity, that's a larger question. Certainly giving people credit for originality, encouraging it, and giving kids some way of reflecting on whether these new ideas are more effective than existing ideas is a powerful part of pedagogy. But you can't reduce everything to a number in the end, and I don't think we should. (p. 26)

The argument against grading creativity is not limited to not reducing everything to a number. Another problem is that, in order to grade, you need criteria and a scale. By definition, if the student has a truly new idea or new product, you can't have already listed all the elements of it you would observe and the criteria by which you would evaluate them. So you don't have a solid basis on which to grade.

However, if you believe that creativity comprises both having a new idea and evaluating the value of the new idea, then it is possible to grade an assignment. Both the *Julius Caesar* and the *Childless Millionaire* assignments that follow are examples of this kind of assignment. These assignments embody the kind of creativity we discussed in Chapter 2. In Bloom's original taxonomy, this was called Synthesis. Anderson and Krathwohl use the word Create, and they mean it in the sense of both creative and critical thinking. Writing an appropriate original ending to a story, for example, requires reasoning and reflection (what do I know about the characters, plot, and setting already in place?), creative production (writing the ending), and evaluation (how well does this ending fit with the characters, plot, and setting already in place?) by the student.

The rest of this chapter gives some examples of how to stimulate and assess creativity. I also try to give some examples of how to refocus the kind of "creativity rubrics" that jeopardize good assessment, so that these, too, become opportunities for creativity.

Assessing Creative Thinking

The very best way to stimulate creativity is to inspire it by making assignments that are, in their own right, creative. The two assignments presented in this section are examples. To assess creative thinking, an assessment should do the following:

• Require student production of some new ideas or a new product, or require students to reorganize existing ideas in some new way. Juxtaposing two different content areas or texts is one way to do this.

• Allow for student choice (which itself can be a "creation of an idea") on matters related to the learning targets(s) to be assessed, not on tangential aspects of the assessment like format.

• If graded, evaluate student work against the criteria students were trying to reach, where appropriate, as well as conventional criteria for real work in the discipline.

Students often receive open-ended assignments, which allow for many good ways to do a successful project. The directions for any project or paper are more or less constraining, more or less open to divergent student responses. The trick is to make your assignment directions specific enough that they require working on the learning target or targets, yet open-ended enough to leave room for student-generated ideas.

To foster creativity in an assignment, the student-generated ideas need to be about the learning target, not about tangential things like format. Teachers sometimes mistakenly restrict student choices to aspects of an assignment that don't really matter. For example, giving students the opportunity to decorate a cover any way they want on a paper about the big bang theory of the origin of the universe does not help students develop a creative, generative approach to science. Giving students the opportunity to approach the material in different ways (for example, as if they were a reporter for the science section of *Parade* magazine, as if they were a high school science teacher, as if they were a NASA administrator, as if they were the parent of a curious child, or other perspectives of their choice) allows students to write very different papers about the big bang and gets creative juices flowing about the topic, not the tangent.

English Example

A 10th grade English teacher gave an assignment as a wrap-up to reading Shakespeare's *Julius Caesar*. Her assignment was intended to be creative in two senses: (1) as the Create level of cognitive activity and (2) in the sense of putting things together in a new way. The teacher got the idea to do a newsletter from several Internet lesson-planning sites. The teacher added some original self-assessment checklists, which she titled, "Deadline approaching—Do a double-check!" for students to use as they prepared their work.

The main creative mechanism in this assignment was juxtaposing two literary forms, Shakespearean tragedy and contemporary newspapers. The directions asked students to develop a front page of a "newspaper" from 44 BC. Students were asked to include the various parts of a newspaper—banner headline, picture with caption, lead story, related stories in sidebars, advertisements, and so on. Students were told they would be evaluated on their

understanding of the plot and characters of Julius Caesar as well as the historical facts surrounding Caesar's rise and fall.

The assignment directions asked students to be creative, but the request
was in the context of an assignment that was clearly about demonstrating
understanding of the plot and characters in *Julius Caesar*. The grading rubrics
carried this through, as well, giving more points to content than to creativity.

An important thing to note about this assignment is that the requested
creativity was grounded. Students put together elements from two unlike
things, a modern-day newspaper and a Shakespeare play, after they had the
opportunity to examine and learn about the elements of both. The project was
the culmination of a unit on *Julius Caesar*, and on the day the assignment was
given, students looked at real newspapers in class in order to become familiar
with elements like headline, index, advertisement, and so on. Both genres,
newspaper and play, were important more broadly as objects of understanding
in the discipline of English/language arts. The point here is that while students
were expected to be creative, the teacher provided resources and inspiration
for that creativity that were discipline-appropriate, educationally sound, and
interesting, too.

The teacher wrote, "My 10th grade English students enjoyed this fun wrap-
up to *Julius Caesar*. They particularly enjoyed the novelty of advertisements—
I had ads for McCaesar's and Toga Rentals. I'm sure they enjoyed the project
more than they did the play itself!" Well, maybe, but it is worth pointing out
that there would have been no project without the play, and no humor either.
"Toga Rentals" is only funny if you know what togas are in their real context.

One particularly successful and creative student titled her newspaper *The
Ambition Weekly*, thus demonstrating her knowledge of the theme of the play.
The feature article summarized the plot very clearly but was written as news
coverage of the assassination. There were humorous advertisements and sidebars ("Caesar's sandals to be sold on eBay"). The creativity in this student's
work was real, grounded in deep understanding—and also just plain fun. The
creative aspects of her work were an integral part of her understanding, not
"fluff" on the edges of it. The rubric the teacher used for assessing this assignment was as follows:

Front Page News Rubric

_____/30   Includes required elements (nameplate, headline, lead story, related story, photo with caption, index, and advertisement) packaged in a "realistic" manner

_____/30   Lead story and other supporting information demonstrates an understanding of plot detail, character, conflicts, and other literary elements illustrated by Shakespeare's play

_____/15   Creativity and professionalism of finished product—error-free, thoughtful presentation

_____/75   Total

Comments:

Creativity was thus worth 20 percent of the final grade. Points allocated to creativity were grounded in the purpose of the assessment—ascertaining thoughtful understanding of *Julius Caesar*.

It is worth noting that the same teacher also tried this newsletter idea in her unit on *To Kill a Mockingbird*, and it did not go over nearly as well. She said the students found writing newsletters about the Great Depression era more like a history project than a response to literature. Students were more creative for their newsletters from 44 BC. If you think about the task from the students' point of view, this situation makes sense. They had studied 20th century U.S. history, and they felt more obligation to get the facts right. It's not that there was any less "history" in 44 BC than in the 1930s, just that students felt less constrained by it. They felt freer to play with anachronisms and to make puns. They didn't feel obliged to think "this didn't really happen" about 44 BC the way they did about the 1930s.

Art Example

Figure 6.1 (p. 136) shows another example of an assignment that requires creativity, this time in art. Several features of the assignment encourage creativity. Students have direct choice about matters that reflect the learning targets of interpreting the painting, understanding the painting in relation to history and culture, and applying appropriate media and techniques to create a painting.

Figure 6.1 ✳ **Art Assignment Requiring Creativity**

This painting, by Georgian artist Niko Pirosmani (1862–1918), was painted around 1900. From the list of questions below, select at least one that you would like to pursue. You may work on several of the questions if you wish.

Childless Millionaire and a Poor Woman Blessed with Children
Niko Pirosmani, c. 1900, public domain

1. This painting is an example of a style of painting called Primitivism. Find out what you can about this style of painting.

   a. Describe the characteristics of the painting that make it an example of Primitivism.

   b. Paint your own Primitive painting. Describe the characteristics of your painting that make it a Primitive, and how you decided to use them in your work.

2. The artist is communicating a message in this painting. What is the message?

    a. Explain how elements of the painting communicate this message. Do you agree with the artist's message? Explain why or why not.

    b. Paint your own painting that communicates a message. Explain how your painting conveys this message.

3. This painting was painted at the turn of the 20th century. Find out what life was like in Georgia (a country on the Black Sea, just south of Russia) at that time. If you can, find out about the artist's life, too.

    a. How does the painting reflect the times? In what ways does the painting reflect the artist's life?

    b. Paint your own painting that reflects the beginning of the 21st century. If you can, incorporate some aspects of your own life in the painting. Explain how your painting shows these things.

If you choose more than one question, you only need to do one painting. For example, if you choose Questions 1 and 2, paint a Primitive that also communicates a message.

CRITERIA for feedback or rubrics for written answers (part a *of each question):*

- Clear, appropriate thesis that answers the question.
- Appropriateness, completeness, and accuracy of evidence from art or history.
- Soundness of reasoning and clarity of explanation.

CRITERIA for feedback or rubrics for paintings and explanations (part b *of each question):*

- Painting with artistic elements (color, style, etc.) consistent with student's intentions for the piece.
- Clear, appropriate statement of what the painting set out to do.
- Soundness of reasoning and clarity of explanation about about how painting serves the intended purpose.

The main creative mechanism in this assignment is that the questions are cross-disciplinary, combining art with history and culture, so the questions themselves invite putting ideas together. Although each question emphasizes one aspect of the painting (asking about the style, the message, and the historical context, respectively), each question also requires making at least some connections among them. Some creative work is required just to answer part *a* of each question. Part *b* of each question requires students to create an original artwork, using the framework they have just articulated for part *a*.

Students' written answers would be assessed on how well they analyzed the artistic style, message, or historical context in regard to the painting. Students' production (creation) of their original painting would not be assessed on how good a painting they had produced, but on how successfully they had fulfilled the requirements of their own analysis. For example, if they said Primitivism required simple figures—were their figures simple?

Formative and Summative Uses of Results

Both the *Julius Caesar* and the *Childless Millionaire* assessments are major projects. As such, they would eventually be assessed summatively, for a grade. Both of these large projects would best be done with formative assessment opportunities built in to various phases of the work. For example, in the *Childless Millionaire* project, students could be asked to do statements of intent describing which questions they were going to choose, and why. They could produce drafts of the written portions of the selected question or questions, which could be the basis for self-assessment, peer assessment, and teacher feedback. They could produce sketches and studies for their paintings. It would squander opportunities for learning, and for improvement, to give either of these assignments solely for summative assessment at a due date.

Revising Grading Schemes and Rubrics That Trivialize Creativity

I hope many readers will have seen that lots of assessments teachers use that have the word *creativity* in the rubric aren't really about assessing creativity at all. They are mislabeled because of misconceptions the teachers may have about what it means to be creative. The most common misconception I have noted in my own work with teachers is saying *creative* when they mean *artistic* or *aesthetically pleasing*. Another common misconception is to use *creativity* to mean *interesting* (to the teacher or reader).

Missing the Point with "Creativity Points"

Some scoring schemes for assignments allot points for creativity that only take away from the purpose of the assignment. One teacher, for example, asked her high school social studies students to do a project on countries. The assignment was done in pairs, and the students had library time. The assignment directions asked students to look up specific information (location, form of government, climate, flora and fauna, major industries and resources, major religions, capital, and so on) and then present it on posters. The format of the poster was specified. For example, the poster title was to be the country name written in capital letters. The scheme for grading was as follows:

Information/content	10 points
Creativity	10 points
Directions followed	10 points

This assessment is a contradiction in terms, allocating one-third of the points for creativity in an assignment that is about finding and reporting on a predetermined list of facts. For this assignment, it's easy to see what's wrong. When asked, this teacher was able to say that for this assignment, by *creativity* she meant that the poster was colorful and appealing to the eye. This is actually not creativity as we have been using the term in this chapter. Using large readable letters, bright colors, and illustrations on the poster are not "new" ideas students would have.

This teacher should, at a minimum, relabel the creativity points and instead say something like "poster is colorful and appealing to the eye." She should also reallocate the point values to reflect the learning target better, making content more important.

I would suggest totally revising this assignment, however. Revise the directions so the students have to do more than list and illustrate facts about a country, which really amounts to little more than finding and outlining an encyclopedia entry. The potential value of this assignment is not really about being creative as we have used the term, but more about analysis. If the teacher had posed analytical questions to students about their country for them to answer—for example, "How do the major industries in the country reflect opportunities afforded by the climate or geopolitical location of the country?"—students would have had to use higher-order thinking of the kind we discussed in Chapter 3.

The misuse of *creativity* in scoring schemes is very common, and often not as obvious as in the first example. Suppose a term paper assignment, in any subject, had a grading scheme like this—much better than the first example but still not a good use of *creativity*:

Content	20 points
Organization	20 points
Creativity	10 points

If *content* meant accuracy and completeness of information, as it often does in term paper assignments, and if *creativity* meant using higher-order thinking to discuss the content, and also that the paper was presented in a neat, aesthetically pleasing way, perhaps even illustrated, then a better way to assess what was really intended would be to start with the assignment. Make sure it really asks a question that requires student thinking, or that it requires students to come up with their own research question and not just a topic (e.g., sound waves, India, Chaucer). Then revise the grading scheme to reflect this:

Thesis clear and supported	20 points
Content accuracy	20 points
Organization of paper	10 points
Presentation	5 points (or 0 points—not graded, just for feedback)

Mis-Specifying Creativity in a Rubric

The first two examples were about misuses of *creativity* in point-based grading schemes, which are very commonly used for projects. This final example is about a creativity rubric used as one of several criteria in a set of analytical rubrics where each scale had four levels. The assignment was to write a review of one of the plays that a class had read in a unit on drama. The creativity portion of the rubric read as follows:

4—Review demonstrated a high level of creativity. It was exciting and interesting. The review made you want to go see the play.

3—Review demonstrated a moderate level of creativity. It was interesting. The review made you want to go see the play.

2—Review demonstrated some level of creativity. It might have been more interesting. The review did not make you want to go see the play.

1—Review demonstrated no level of creativity. It was not interesting. The review did not make you want to go see the play.

Reading the rubric, it seems clear that what the teacher meant to assess included two qualities: interest and persuasiveness of writing. Further, it is quite likely that the focus on interest (and excitement, in Level 4) was included because making the play sound interesting would help readers want to go see it. In this case, then, the teacher could have revised the rubric using any one of a number of persuasive-writing rubrics, or written her own. Even changing *creativity* to *persuasion* and otherwise using the rubric as is would have been clearer.

It may seem like I have spent a lot of time in this "what not to do" section of the chapter on creativity. Readers will have noticed I didn't do that in other chapters. I hope that these examples will help refocus assessment of creativity that really means something else (neatness, artistry, interest, persuasiveness, and so on) to its true target. I further hope that these negative examples, coming after the discussion of creativity in its true sense, will help recapture the term to mean the important 21st century skill of generating and subsequently evaluating new ideas or products.

Summing Up

In this chapter, I have discussed what creativity is and how it might be assessed. Creativity is a very important goal, and we do it a disservice when we trivialize it. Anyone can be creative and should be encouraged in this area. Creativity is a human skill, and the advancement of civilization depends on it.

The basics required for creativity include a deep knowledge base in a subject and a willingness to play with the ideas in new ways. These are the characteristics of the educated and flexible citizens we all hope students will become for the 21st century. They are also the characteristics of those who have brought us to the 21st century, from the inventor of the wheel to the present time.

Afterword

When students receive instruction in higher-order thinking skills, they perform better on a whole range of measures, from large-scale standardized tests to classroom tasks. Students who are regularly and routinely challenged to think, and whose teachers assess higher-order thinking in a manner that yields useful information for both students and teachers in their pursuit of improvement, will learn to think well.

This conclusion is no surprise, but as we have seen in this book, it takes intentional work to make these things happen in the classroom. Extemporaneous classroom discussion questions tend to be recall-level questions: "Who can tell me who Abraham Lincoln was?" Assessing higher-order thinking doesn't mean you don't assess knowledge of facts and concepts, too. But it is easier to assess recall than it is to assess thinking, so in this book we have concentrated on the assessment of thinking. I hope this book has helped you see how to construct higher-order-thinking questions and tasks, in two ways.

First, I hope that separating out different aspects of higher-order thinking has functioned as a sort of analysis to help you "think about thinking." In this Afterword, let me draw the threads back together and remind you that there was a lot of overlap among these aspects of thinking. There is good thinking and bad thinking, of course, but the categories we used in this book are not rigidly different kinds of thinking.

Rather than defining "types" of thinking, I intended the structure of this book to be of heuristic value. A heuristic is a helpful way of thinking about something, a pattern for learning, or a model for solving a problem. Bloom's taxonomy was conceived in that vein—not as a rigid set of categories but as a helpful way of thinking about instructional intentions, giving teachers ways to think about expanding their instruction beyond facts. The chapters in this book were intended to help you think about different ways students can be asked to think, sort of in answer to the question "What does higher-order thinking look like?"

Second, I hope that this book has answered the question "How do I assess higher-order thinking?" Certain principles are important for all assessment: (1) clearly specify what it is you want to assess, (2) design a task or test item that requires students to do precisely that, and (3) decide how you will interpret and evaluate the results. Assessing higher-order thinking requires some additional principles: (4) use introductory material or allow access to resource material, (5) use novel material, and (6) attend separately to cognitive complexity and difficulty.

The bulk of the book has been devoted to working out these principles in specific strategies for assessment questions and tasks that tap the various aspects of higher-order thinking. These specific strategies are summarized in Figure A.1 (pp. 144–147).

Figure A.1 * Specific Strategies for Assessing Higher-Order Thinking

To Assess How Well Students Can . . .	Provide This Kind of Material . . .	And Ask Students To . . .
Focus on a question or identify the main idea	A text, speech, problem, policy, political cartoon, or experiment and results	• Identify the main issue, the main idea, or the problem, and explain their reasoning
Analyze arguments	A text, speech, or experimental design	• Identify what evidence the author gives that supports (or contradicts) the argument • Identify assumptions that must be true to make the argument valid • Explain the logical structure of the argument (including identifying irrelevancies, if they exist)
Compare and contrast	Two texts, events, scenarios, concepts, characters, or principles	• Identify elements in each • Organize the elements according to whether they are alike or different
Evaluate materials and methods for their intended purposes	A text, speech, policy, theory, experimental design, work of art	• Identify the purpose the author or designer was trying to accomplish • Identify elements in the work • Judge the value of those elements for accomplishing the intended purpose • Explain their reasoning
Put unlike things together in a new way	A complex task or problem	• Generate multiple solutions OR • Plan a procedure OR • Produce something new

To Assess How Well Students Can . . .	Provide This Kind of Material . . .	And Ask Students To . . .
Assess their own work (self-assess)	A set of clear criteria and one or more examples of their own work	• Identify elements in their own work • Evaluate these elements against the criteria • Devise a plan to improve
Make or evaluate a deductive conclusion	Statement or premises	• Draw a logical conclusion and explain their reasoning OR • Select a logical conclusion from a set of choices OR • Identify a counter-example that renders the statement untrue
Make or evaluate an inductive conclusion	A statement or scenario and information in the form of a graph, table, chart, or list	• Draw a logical conclusion and explain their reasoning OR • Select a logical conclusion from a set of choices
Evaluate the credibility of a source	A scenario, speech, advertisement, Web site or other source of information	• Decide what portion of the information is believable, and explain their reasoning
Identify implicit assumptions	An argument, speech, or explanation that has some implicit assumptions	• Explain what must be assumed (taken for granted) in order for the argument or explanation to make sense OR • Select an implicit assumption from a set of choices

continued

Figure A.1 ✳ **Specific Strategies for Assessing Higher-Order Thinking** *(continued)*

To Assess How Well Students Can . . .	Provide This Kind of Material . . .	And Ask Students To . . .
Identify rhetorical and persuasive strategies	A speech, advertisement, editorial, or other persuasive communication	• Identify elements of the communication that are intended to persuade, and explain why • Identify any statements or strategies that are intentionally misleading, and explain why
Identify or define a problem	A scenario or problem description	• Identify the problem that needs to be solved OR • Identify the question that needs to be answered
Identify irrelevancies to solving a problem	A scenario or problem description that may include some irrelevant material	• Identify the elements that are relevant and irrelevant to solving the problem, and explain their reasoning
Describe and evaluate multiple solution strategies	A scenario or problem description	• Solve the problem in two or more ways • Prioritize solutions and explain their reasoning
Model a problem	A scenario or problem description	• Draw or diagram the problem situation
Identify obstacles to solving a problem	A scenario or problem description	• Explain why the problem is difficult • Describe obstacles to solving the problem • Identify additional information needed for solving the problem

To Assess How Well Students Can . . .	Provide This Kind of Material . . .	And Ask Students To . . .
Reason with data	A text, cartoon, graph, data table, or chart and a problem that requires this information for its solution	• Solve the problem and explain their reasoning
Use analogies	A scenario or problem description (and possibly a solution strategy)	• Solve the problem and explain how the solution would apply to other scenarios or problems OR • Explain how the solution would apply to other scenarios or problems
Solve a problem backward	A scenario or problem description and a desired end state or solution	• Plan a strategy to get to the end state from the problem statement OR • Describe how to reason backward from the solution to the question
Think creatively	A complex problem or task that requires either brainstorming new ideas or reorganizing existing ideas or a problem with no currently known solution	• Produce something original OR • Organize existing material in new ways OR • Reframe a question or problem in a different way

In the book I have given examples from a range of content areas and grade levels and invited you to apply the strategies to your own teaching. Thus I hope this book has made it easier for you to assess higher-order thinking in your classroom.

For each assessment example, I have listed criteria for appraisal. You always need criteria for sound assessment (Principle 3 above), whether you are assessing for formative or summative purposes, and whether you are giving feedback, scoring, or both. In your own work, plan the criteria at the same time you plan the assessment questions or tasks. Use the criteria to focus your feedback, student self-evaluation, or student peer evaluation, as appropriate. Use the same criteria for constructing the scoring rubrics you need, which will differ according to the scope of the assignment and its fit in your overall grading scheme.

Thinking is a teachable and learnable skill and should not be reserved, as some misconstrue, for high achievers only. Teachers can expect, teach, and assess thinking skills for all students. Reflect on your own practice. Where your instruction and assessment are heavy on recall and comprehension, figure out ways to extend them into the realm of higher-order thinking.

As you assess students' thinking, you will get information about strengths and weaknesses in their thinking patterns. Give feedback about both. Where student thinking is strong, name and describe for students what they did. They won't know you noticed unless you tell them, and talking about their thinking will give them language with which to understand it and, ultimately, to regulate it themselves. Where student thinking is weak, walk them through the process. Model for them what clear thinking would look like on a particular type of task or question. Then give them another similar kind of thinking task to try, give feedback on that, and so on.

Most students actually *like* to think. Most students would be absolutely delighted to be able to show you what they know by doing assignments and assessments that require higher-order thinking. Well-designed assessments bring thinking "out of the kids' heads" and make it visible in students' words, writing, and products. Work that makes cognitive complexity, reasoning, judgment, problem solving, and creativity visible allows both teachers and students to describe and appraise students' thinking, and to think together about what to tackle next. Once students learn to see problems in ordinary things, as the MacArthur grant recipient Lakshminarayanan Mahadevan does, there is always something else to think about.

✳ | References

Anderson, L. W., & Krathwohl, D. R. (Eds.). (2001). *A taxonomy for learning, teaching, and assessing: A revision of Bloom's Taxonomy of Educational Objectives* (Complete ed.). New York: Longman.

Andrade, H. L., Du, Y., & Wang, X. (2008). Putting rubrics to the test: The effect of a model, criteria generation, and rubric-referenced self-assessment on elementary students' writing. *Educational Measurement: Issues and Practice, 27*(2), 3–13.

Arem, G. (2006). Using student assessments in archery to increase higher-order thinking and student success. *Strategies, 19*(4), 34–38.

Ayres, P. L. (1993). Why goal-free problems can facilitate learning. *Contemporary Educational Psychology, 18*(3), 376–381.

Azzam, A. (2009). Why creativity now? A conversation with Sir Ken Robinson. *Educational Leadership, 67*(1), 22–26.

Barahal, S. L. (2008). Thinking about thinking. *Phi Delta Kappan, 90*(4), 298–302.

Biggs, J. B., & Collis, K. F. (1982). *Evaluating the quality of learning: The SOLO taxonomy.* New York: Academic Press.

Bloom, B. S., Engelhart, M. D., Furst, E. J., Hill, W. H., & Krathwohl, D. R. (1956). *Taxonomy of educational objectives: The classification of educational goals. Handbook I: Cognitive domain.* White Plains, NY: Longman.

Bransford, J. D., & Stein, B. S. (1984). *The IDEAL problem solver.* New York: W. H. Freeman.

Carroll, L., & Leander, S. (2001). *Improving student motivation through the use of active learning strategies.* Unpublished thesis, Saint Xavier University, Chicago. ERIC Document No. ED455961.

Higgins, S., Hall, E., Baumfield, V., & Moseley, D. (2005). A meta-analysis of the impact of the implementation of thinking skills approaches on pupils. In *Research evidence in education library*. London: EPPI-Centre, Social Science Research Unit, Institute of Education, University of London.

Kuhlthau, C. C. (2005). Towards collaboration between information seeking and information retrieval. *Information Research, 10*(2), paper 225. Retrieved May 13, 2009, from http://informationr.net/ir/10-2/paper225.html

Marso, R. N., & Pigge, F. L. (1993). Teachers' testing knowledge, skills, and practice. In S. L. Wise (Ed.), *Teacher training in measurement and assessment skills* (pp. 129–185). Lincoln, NE: Buros Institute of Mental Measurements.

Marzano, R. J., & Kendall, J. S. (2007). *The new taxonomy of educational objectives* (2nd ed.). Thousand Oaks, CA: Sage.

Marzano, R. J., Pickering, D., & McTighe, J. (1993). *Assessing student outcomes: Performance assessment using the dimensions of learning model.* Alexandria, VA: ASCD.

McClymer, J. F., & Knoles, L. Z. (1992). Ersatz learning, inauthentic testing. *Journal on Excellence in College Teaching, 3*, 33–50.

McMillan, J. H. (2001). Secondary teachers' classroom assessment and grading practices. *Educational Measurement: Issues and Practice, 20*(1), 20–32.

McMillan, J. H., Myron, S., & Workman, D. (2002). Elementary teachers' classroom assessment and grading practices. *Journal of Educational Research, 95*, 203–213.

Meece, J. L. (2003). Applying learner-centered principles to middle school education. *Theory into Practice, 42*(2), 109–116.

Meece, J. L., & Miller, S. D. (1999). Changes in elementary school children's achievement goals for reading and writing: Results of a longitudinal and an intervention study. *Scientific Studies of Reading, 3*, 207–229.

National Public Radio. (2009, September 22). *The 2009 winners of MacArthur "genius grants."* Retrieved October 5, 2009, from http://www.npr.org/templates/story/story.php?storyId=113088249

Newmann, F. M., Bryk, A. S., & Nagaoka, J. K. (2001, January). *Authentic intellectual work and standardized tests: Conflict or coexistence?* Chicago: Consortium on Chicago School Research.

Nitko, A. J., & Brookhart, S. M. (2007). *Educational assessment of students* (5th ed.). Upper Saddle River, NJ: Pearson Education.

Norris, S. P., & Ennis, R. H. (1989). *Evaluating critical thinking.* Pacific Grove, CA: Critical Thinking Press & Software.

Partnership for 21st Century Skills. (2009, May). *P21 framework definitions document.* Retrieved September 9, 2009, from http://www.p21.org/documents/P21_Framework_Definitions.pdf

Pogrow, S. (2005). HOTS revisited: A thinking development approach to reducing the learning gap after grade 3. *Phi Delta Kappan, 87*(1), 64–75.

Ross, J. A., Hogaboam-Gray, A., & Rolheiser, C. (2002). Student self-evaluation in grade 5–6 mathematics: Effects on problem-solving achievement. *Educational Assessment, 8*(1), 43–58.

Sweller, J. (2009). Cognitive bases of human creativity. *Educational Psychology Review, 21*(1), 11–19.

Webb, N. L. (2002). *Alignment study in language arts, mathematics, science and social studies of state standards and assessments for four states.* Washington, DC: Council of Chief State School Officers.

Wenglinsky, H. (2004). Facts or critical thinking skills? What NAEP results say. *Educational Leadership, 62*(1), 32–35.

 Index

Information in figures is indicated by *f*.

acceptability, social, 67*f*
achievement
    assessment and, 9–10
    evidence of, 24
    thinking-skills interventions and, 9
ad hominem, 67*f*
Aesop, 26–29
algebraic proofs, 73
analogy
    in problem solving, 119–120
    reasoning by, 65, 78–81, 147*f*
analysis
    of arguments or theses, 46–49, 144*f*
    assessment of, 42–52
    in cognitive taxonomy, 40, 41
    compare and contrast in, 49–52
    main ideas and, 43–46
    "means-end," 120
"Androcles and the Lion" (Aesop), 26–29
appeal to authority, 67*f*
application, in cognitive taxonomy, 40, 41
arguments
    against person, 67*f*

arguments (*continued*)
    analysis of, 46–49, 144*f*
    straw man, 67*f*
"Artful Thinking Palette," 6
assessment. *See also* tests
    achievement and, 9–10
    of analogy-based reasoning, 147*f*
    of analysis, 42–52
    of argument analysis, 46–49, 144*f*
    of assumption identification, 145*f*
    of backward problem solving, 147*f*
    balance of content and thinking in, 20,
        23–24
    blueprint, 20–23, 21*f*–22*f*
    clarity in target of, 19
    cognitive complexity *vs.* difficulty in, 29
    compare and contrast in, 49–52, 51*f*
    of compare and contrast skills, 144*f*
    complexity in, 29
    constructed-response questions in,
        33–35
    of creation, 55–56
    of creative thinking, 131–138, 147*f*

assessment. *See also* tests (*continued*)
 of credibility evaluation, 145*f*
 of data-based reasoning, 147*f*
 of deduction, 145*f*
 difficulty in, 29
 effect of, 8–13
 essay questions in summative, 33–35
 of evaluation, 53–55, 144*f*
 evidence in, 24
 feedback in, 30–37
 formative, 31–33, 32*f*, 45–46, 57–58,
  81–82
 goal identification in, 18–19
 introductory material in, 25
 of judgment, 86–96
 of logic, 68–81, 80*f*–81*f*
 of modeling, 146*f*
 motivation and, 12–13
 multiple-choice questions in, 33
 novel material in, 25–29
 of obstacle identification, 146*f*
 performance task design in, 19–24
 of persuasion identification, 146*f*
 principles of, 17–29
 of problem identification, 146*f*
 of problem solving, 102–121, 147*f*
 of reasoning, 68–81, 80*f*–81*f*
 of rhetoric identification, 146*f*
 scoring in, 30–37
 self, 58–59, 145*f*
 summative, 33–37, 35*f*, 57–58, 81–82
 of thesis analysis, 46–49
 of writing *vs.* thinking, 50–52
assumptions, 62–63, 88–91, 145*f*
authority, appeal to, 67*f*
avoidance, work, 12–13

backward problem solving, 120–121, 147*f*
balance, of content and thinking, 20, 23–24
Bloom's taxonomy, 5, 39. *See also*
 taxonomy(ies), cognitive
blueprint, assessment, 20–23, 21*f*–22*f*

book report, 53–54
brainstorming, 130–131

checklists, self-assessment, 59
Childless Millionaire example, 135–138
choice, in creative thinking assessment, 132
clumps, information, 105
cognitive complexity, difficulty *vs.*, 29
cognitive taxonomies. *See* taxonomy(ies),
 cognitive
compare and contrast, 49–52, 51*f*, 144*f*
complexity, difficulty *vs.*, 29
comprehension, in cognitive taxonomy, 40
conclusion
 deductive, 68–74, 145*f*
 inductive, 74–81, 145*f*
 reasoning to, 63
constructed-response questions, 33–35
creativity / creative thinking
 in art, 135–138
 assessment of, 55–56, 131–138, 147*f*
 brainstorming and, 130–131
 in cognitive taxonomy, 41
 definition of, 124–130
 in English, 133–135
 evaluation and, 126
 as evaluative, 126–127
 as generative, 125–126, 126–127
 misspecification of, 140–141
 in Partnership for 21st Century Skills,
  127–128
 "points," 138–140
 in problem solving, 129–130
 productivity and, 125
 promotion of, 130–131
 reflectivity and, 126
 requirements for, 128–129
 trivialization of, 138–141
credibility, 6, 85–86, 86–88, 145*f*
critical thinking
 definition of, 84
 higher-order thinking as, 4, 5–6

Danka, Robert, 31
data
    in problem solving, 115–119
    reasoning from, 64–65, 115–119, 147*f*
deduction, 62–63
deductive conclusion, 68–74, 145*f*
Depth of Knowledge levels, 41–42
description, of problem-solving strategies,
    106–111
difficulty, cognitive complexity *vs.,* 29
disadvantaged students, HOTS program for,
    11–12
Donne, John, 126

"elevator story," 129
epistemology, 3
errors, logical, 66, 67*f*
essay questions, 33–35
    for deductive conclusions, 70–71
evaluation
    assessment of, 53–55, 144*f*
    in cognitive taxonomy, 40
    in creative thinking, 126–127
    creativity and, 126
    of credibility, 86–88
    of problem-solving strategies, 106–111
evidence, in assessment, 24
examples, reasoning from, 64–65

fable, assessment example with, 26–29
facts, usefulness of, 1
feedback
    in assessment, 30–37
    in formative assessment, 45–46
Fleming, Alexander, 127
Ford City High School, 87
formative assessment, 31–33, 32*f,* 45–46
formative use of results, 57–58
    in creativity, 138–141
    in judgment, 96
    in problem solving, 121–122
    in reasoning, 81–82

generative, creative thinking as, 125–126,
    126–127
"goal-free" problems, 101–102
goals, in assessment, identification of, 18–19
good judgment, 85–86. *See also* judgment

Harvard University, 6
higher-order thinking
    as critical thinking, 4, 5–6
    definition of, 3–8
    neglect of, 1–2
    novel material and, 25–26
    as problem solving, 4, 7–8
    as transfer, 3, 4–5
Higher Order Thinking Skills (HOTS) pro-
    gram, 11–12
HOTS. *See* Higher Order Thinking Skills
    (HOTS) program

IDEAL Problem Solver, 7, 99
"if-then" logic, 64*f*
IGAP. *See* Illinois Goals Assessment Program
    (IGAP)
Illinois Goals Assessment Program (IGAP),
    10
implicit assumptions, 88, 145*f*
induction, 63–65
inductive conclusion, 74–81
information, searching for, 104
interactive instruction, 11
interventions, thinking-skills, 8–9
introductory material, in assessment, 25
Iowa Tests of Basic Skills (ITBS), 10–11
irrelevancies
    assessment of identification of, 146*f*
    in problem solving, 104–106
ITBS. *See* Iowa Tests of Basic Skills (ITBS)

judgment
    assessment of, 86–96
    assumption identification and, 88–91
    of credibility, 85–86, 86–88

judgment (*continued*)
    definition of, 85–86
    good, 85–86
    knowledge and, 6
    multiple-choice question assessment
        of, 88–89
    persuasive strategies and, 91–96
    rhetorical strategies and, 91–96
    rubric for, 92*f*
    types of, 84
    writing in assessment of, 93–94
Julius Caesar (Shakespeare), 133–135
juxtaposition, in creative thinking assessment, 132

KCCT. *See* Kentucky Core Content Test (KCCT)
Kentucky, 37
Kentucky Core Content Test (KCCT), 37
Kittanning High School, 31
knowledge
    in Bloom's cognitive taxonomy, 40
    definition of, 3
    use of, 1–2

learner-centered practices, 13
Lincoln High School, 36
literary criticism, 53
logic. *See also* reasoning
    assessment of, 68–81, 80*f*–81*f*
    errors in, 66, 67*f*
    "if-then," 64*f*
logs, reader-response, 131

MacArthur Foundation, 130
Mahadevan, Lakshminarayanan, 129–130
main idea, 43–46, 46*f*
Marshall Plan performance assessment, 81–82
Mathematics Problem-Solving Scoring Guide, 36
McCausland, Patti, 50

"means-end analysis," 120
Melville, Herman, 25–26
memory
    cognitive taxonomy and, 41
    speed in, 1
Moby Dick (Melville), 25–26
modeling
    assessment of, 146*f*
    in problem solving, 111–112
motivation
    assessment and, 12–13
    thinking-skills interventions and, 9
Mulroy, Patrick, 87
multiple-choice questions, 33
    for deductive conclusions, 70
    for judgment assessment, 88–89

NAEP. *See* National Assessment of Educational Progress (NAEP)
National Assessment of Educational Progress (NAEP), 10
newsletter project, 133–135
novel material, in assessment, 25–29

obstacles, in problem solving, 112–115, 146*f*
off-task time, 13
overgeneralization, 67*f*

Partnership for 21st Century Skills, 127–128
penicillin, 127
Pennsylvania System of School Assessment (PSSA) test, 31
perceptions, of learner-centered practices, 13
performance assessments
    for deductive conclusions, 71–72
    Marshall Plan, 81–82
    in summative assessment, 35–37
performance tasks, design of, 19–24
persuasive strategies
    identification of, 91–96, 146*f*
    in science, 94–95

philosophy, 3
Plato, 3
premises, 62–63
problem solving
    additional information for, identification of need of, 112–115
    analogies in, 119–120
    assessment of, 102–121
    backward, 120–121, 147*f*
    creativity in, 129–130
    data in reasoning with, 115–119
    definition of, 98–100
    description of strategies in, 106–111
    "goal-free" problems in, 101–102
    higher-order thinking as, 4, 7–8
    IDEAL model for, 7, 99
    identification of problem in, 102–103
    irrelevancies in, 104–106, 146*f*
    modeling in, 111–112
    multiple strategies in, 106–111
    obstacle identification in, 112–115, 146*f*
    rubrics, 36–37, 99
    structured *vs.* unstructured problems in, 100–101
    types of problems in, 100–102
productivity, creativity and, 125
Project Zero, 6
promotion, of creativity, 130–131
proofs, algebraic, 73
PSSA. *See* Pennsylvania System of School Assessment (PSSA) test

questions
    constructed-response, 33–35
    essay, 33–35
        for deductive conclusions, 70–72
    focusing on, 43–46
    multiple-choice, 33
        for deductive conclusions, 70
        for judgment assessment, 88–89
reader-response logs, 131
reasoning. *See also* logic
    by analogy, 65, 78–81

reasoning. *See also* logic (*continued*)
    assessment of, 68–81, 80*f*–81*f*
    assumptions and, 62–63
    to conclusion, 63
    from data, 64–65, 147*f*
    deduction in, 62–63
    definition of, 62–66, 67*f*
    development of, 61
    early learning of, 61
    errors in, 66, 67*f*
    from examples, 64–65
    by induction, 74–78
    induction in, 63–65
    from other information, 64–65
    premises and, 62–63
    skills in, 65–66
    sound, 62–66, 67*f*
recall, 1–2
reflectivity, 126
relevancy, in problem solving, 104–106
requirements, for creativity, 128–129
rhetorical strategies, identification of, 91–96, 146*f*
Robinson, Sir Ken, 126, 131
rubric(s)
    balance of content and thinking for, 23–24
    creativity in, misspecification of, 140–141
    critical thinking, 92*f*
    for main idea, 46*f*
    problem-solving, 36–37, 99
    self-assessment, 59
    for written projects, 80*f*–81*f*

science, persuasive tactics in, 94–95
scoring, in assessment, 30–37
searching, for information, 104
self-assessment, 58–59, 145*f*
Shakespeare, William, 48
shapes, information, 105
skills, general reasoning, 65–66
skits, 56

social acceptability, logical error and, 67*f*
SOLO Taxonomy, 42
Sonnet 149 (Shakespeare), 48
sound reasoning, 62–66, 67*f. See also*
    reasoning
source credibility, 6, 86–88
spelling, 52
straw man argument, 67*f*
structured problems, 100–101
students, self-assessment by, 58–59
summative assessment, 33–37, 35*f*
summative use of results, 57–58
    in creativity, 138–141
    in judgment, 96
    in problem solving, 121–122
    in reasoning, 81–82
synthesis, in cognitive taxonomy, 40, 56

taxonomy(ies), cognitive
    analysis assessment and, 42–52
    analysis in, 40, 41
    application in, 40, 41
    Bloom's, 5, 39
    comprehension in, 40
    creation in, 41
    definition of, 40–42
    evaluation in, 40
    knowledge in, 40
    memory in, 41
    SOLO, 42
    synthesis in, 40, 56
    understanding in, 41
    use of, 39

tests. *See also* assessment
    misconceptions on, 1–2
    recall and, 1–2
Theaetetus (Plato), 3
theses, analysis of, 46–49
thinking-skills interventions, 8–9
time, off-task, 13
TIMSS. *See* Trends in International
    Mathematics and Science Study (TIMSS)
"topic dumping," 104–105
transfer, higher-order thinking as, 3, 4–5
Trends in International Mathematics and
    Science Study (TIMSS), 10
trivialization, of creativity, 138–141

understanding, in cognitive taxonomy, 41
units, balance of content and thinking for, 23
unstructured problems, 100–101

West Hills Intermediate Elementary School,
    50
wisdom, 5–6
work avoidance, 12–13
writing
    assessment of, *vs.* thinking, 50–52
    in judgment assessment, 93–94
    of reader-response logs, 131
    rubrics for, 80*f*–81*f*
    of skits, 56

About the Author

Susan M. Brookhart, Ph.D., is an independent educational consultant based in Helena, Montana. She works with ASCD as an ASCD Faculty Member, providing on-site professional development in formative assessment. She has taught both elementary and middle school. She was Professor and Chair of the Department of Educational Foundations and Leadership at Duquesne University, where she currently serves as Senior Research Associate in the Center for Advancing the Study of Teaching and Learning in the School of Education. She serves on the state assessment advisory committee for the state of Montana and on the College Board's Research and Development Advisory Committee. She has been the education columnist for *National Forum*, the journal of Phi Kappa Phi, and Editor of *Educational Measurement: Issues and Practice*, a journal of the National Council on Measurement in Education. She is the author or coauthor of several books, including ASCD's *How to Give Effective Feedback to Your Students* and *Advancing Formative Assessment in Every Classroom: A Guide for Instructional Leaders*. She can be reached at susanbrookhart@bresnan.net.

Related ASCD Resources

At the time of publication, the following ASCD resources were available (ASCD stock numbers appear in parentheses). For up-to-date information about ASCD resources, go to www.ascd.org.

Multimedia

Formative Assessment Strategies for Every Classroom: An ASCD Action Tool by Susan M. Brookhart (#111005)

Networks

Visit the ASCD Web site (www.ascd.org) and click on About ASCD. Go to the section on Networks for information about professional educators who have formed groups around topics such as "Assessment for Learning." Look in the Network Directory for current facilitators' addresses and phone numbers.

Online Courses

Visit the ASCD Web site (www.ascd.org) for the following professional development opportunities:
Designing Performance Assessments (#PD09OC30)
Measurement That's Useful (#PD09OC31)

Print Products

Advancing Formative Assessment in Every Classroom: A Guide for Instructional Leaders by Connie M. Moss and Susan M. Brookhart (#109031)
Checking for Understanding: Formative Assessment Techniques for Your Classroom by Douglas Fisher and Nancy Frey (#107023)
Classroom Assessment and Grading That Work by Robert J. Marzano (#106006)
Improving Student Learning One Teacher at a Time by Jane Pollock (#107005)
Educational Leadership, December 2007/January 2008: Informative Assessment (#108023)
Exploring Formative Assessment (The Professional Learning Community Series) by Susan Brookhart (#109038)
How to Give Effective Feedback to Your Students by Susan M. Brookhart (#108019)
Transformative Assessment by W. James Popham (#108018)
What Teachers Really Need to Know About Formative Assessment by Laura Greenstein (#110017)

Video and DVD

Assessment for 21st Century Learning (Three DVDs, each with a professional development program) (#610010)
Formative Assessment in Content Areas (Three DVDs, each with a professional development program) (#609034)
Giving Effective Feedback to Your Students (Three DVDs, each with a professional development program) (#609035)
The Power of Formative Assessment to Advance Learning (Three DVDs with a comprehensive user guide) (#608066)

For more information, visit us on the World Wide Web (http://www.ascd.org); send an e-mail message to member@ascd.org; call the ASCD Service Center (1-800-933-ASCD or 703-578-9600, then press 2); send a fax to 703-575-5400; or write to Information Services, ASCD, 1703 N. Beauregard St., Alexandria, VA 22311-1714 USA.

 The Whole Child Initiative helps schools and communities create learning environments that allow students to be healthy, safe, engaged, supported, and challenged. To learn more about other books and resources that relate to the whole child, visit www.wholechildeducation.org.